CONGO VIGNETTES

Stories of God's Faithfulness
to Three Generations in
the Heart of Africa

CONGO VIGNETTES

*Stories of God's Faithfulness
to Three Generations in
the Heart of Africa*

Shawn Lantz

Word Entertainment
Nashville, Tennessee

Book cover design, Laban Ministries International logo and prayer card courtesy of Jackie Mayberry, senior designer, at JCI Design of Dearborn, Michigan. www.jcidesign.com

Interior design and typography by Prototype Graphics in Mt. Juliet, Tennessee. Email: prototype@tds.net

Chapter titles, with the exception of "Yesu Azali Awa," translated from English into Kituba by Jim and Nancy Smith.

Photo on book cover: *Dr. Laban Smith with Congolese witchdoctors and villagers renouncing fetishes. Laban's son, Jim, in right foreground wearing hat, circa 1949.*

Author photo on back cover courtesy of Chris Smith. www.chrisandcamiphotography.com

Rob and Shawn Lantz wedding photo courtesy of Barry Bertsch Photography, Chicago, Illinois.

Printed in Canada

1 2 3 4 5 6 7 8 — 14 13 12 11 10 09 08

Acknowledgments

I must thank those who have helped me along the way in the writing of this book. Without them, these stories may have never been written. Profound thanks needs to be given to the following:

To my Lord Jesus Christ: This is my offering. May You alone receive the glory of which You are so worthy. What You open no one can shut, and what You shut no one can open. Thank You for Your presence in my life. You are the reason I get up in the morning. I do not want to go anywhere You do not lead. Help me to continue to trust You and remember the lessons You have taught me through the writing of this book.

To my best friend and husband, Rob: Without your steadfast love and support, this project would have continued to be memories in my mind. Your editing help and computer expertise have been invaluable. You have been the picture of Christ to me in our marriage. Robbie, you are my hero and the greatest gift God has ever given to me. Until death do us part, I will always be your Oondah.

To my three precious children, Chase, Jordyn, and Jenna: You make my life so rich. You three are my teachers and my greatest earthly treasure. Your mama loves you very much.

To my parents, Jim and Nancy Smith: The faithful example of your lives is what makes me believe God is who He says He is and that He has the power to do what He says He can do. Thank you, Mom, for all of your editing help. I love you both more than I can express in words.

To Dad and Mom Lantz: Thank you for wonderful family times in Savannah. May the Lord give us many more together on earth and in heaven. I love you.

To my siblings, Greg and Nicol, Todd and Angie, Jack and Molly, and all my precious nieces and nephews: Thank you for cherished memories, old and new. May we continue to remember who has gone before us. I love you all.

To Uncle Paul, Aunt Gerry, Terri, and Mark: Thank you for the hope and comfort your letters brought us during difficult days in Congo. I love you all very much.

To my beloved Grandpa and Grandma McKown: Although you have both been gone for many years, your faces are the joy of some of my very best childhood memories. Because of our shared faith in Jesus, our earthly good-bye will one day be changed to heaven's hello.

To the Lowe and Duquette families: Karen and Cindy, we are sisters by more than marriage alone. You have my love and friendship always.

To my soul sisters Laura, Deb, and Desiree: Your friendship continues to sharpen me. I love you.

To my Bible study sisters in Franklin: Let's keep doing this life together as we look ahead expectantly to the great things God has for all of us.

To the Voth family, Uncle Lee, Aunt Jody, Pam, and Kevin: Without your loving hearts and obedience in showing hospitality to our weary, bewildered family throughout your time in the D.R.C., *Congo Vignettes* may have never happened. You have my eternal gratefulness and much love.

To Mark Funderburg: Thank you for catching the vision of *Congo Vignettes*. Your integrity, support, and encouragement have given wings to this project.

To the entire Word staff: Somehow God has enabled you to love a people you have never met. The unity we have experienced as coworkers in the gospel is a demonstration of the power of the One we serve. I am unable to thank you adequately.

To Laban and Marcella Smith: Thank you for the legacy and heritage your obedience has given to your descendants. Thank you for doing the hard part of plowing the ground and sowing eternal seed with your prayers and the sacrifice of your lives. I look forward to heaven, knowing you will be there waiting for all of us.

Dedication

T o my dear Congolese brothers and sisters: Thank you for teaching me the true meaning of wealth. I believe Hebrews 11 was written with you in mind. Although you suffer in obscurity, there is a day of reward coming, precious ones!

Then I saw a new heaven and a new earth, for the first heaven and the first earth had passed away, and there was no longer any sea. I saw the Holy City, the new Jerusalem, coming down out of heaven from God, prepared as a bride beautifully dressed for her husband. And I heard a loud voice from the throne saying, "Now the dwelling of God is with men, and he will live with them. They will be his people, and God himself will be with them and be their God. He will wipe every tear from their eyes. There will be no more death or mourning or crying or pain, for the old order of things has passed away." He who was seated on the throne said, "I am making everything new!" Then he said, "Write this down, for these words are trustworthy and true."
—REVELATION 21:1–5

Table of Contents

Author's Note

I am profoundly grateful for those of you who will read these stories of my family's struggles and triumphs. No family is perfect. It has not been my desire to paint a false picture of perfection. Many prayers have been offered throughout the writing of this project that these stories would glorify the Lord Jesus Christ alone. May nothing that has been written glorify ordinary, fallen members of the Smith family.

I must explain that *Congo Vignettes* is not the entire story. The apostle John ends his gospel by noting that Christ's ministry was so voluminous he could not capture every event. While I would never dare to compare a work of human beings to Christ's earthly ministry, I do not know everything that took place in the minds and hearts of my grandparents, Laban and Marcella Smith. I can only see the imprint of their lives mirrored in a people in the Congo and in the life of my father, Jim. Heaven will be a wonderful place to learn the whole story, but the Holy Spirit has been faithful to keep alive the vision of a man and woman who gave everything away to gain and pass down a wonderful legacy to their son and daughter-in-law and their grandchildren.

These vignettes tell the story of three generations. Laban and Marcella Smith started a work seventy years ago that is currently continuing in the lives of my father and mother, Jim and Nancy Smith. Although my three siblings—Nicol, Todd, and Jack—and I never met our grandfather, the answers to prayers that he and my grandmother prayed for us decades before we were born are being realized in our present lives. The New Testament book of James says the fervent prayers of a righteous man avail much.

There are two things I have prayed for you, the reader, during this project. I have asked the Holy Spirit to give you His hope and His comfort as you enter into a world and culture many of you have never experienced. Although many of these stories take place in a country you may have never visited, I do not want that to be an obstacle in any way to your reading experience. I have no power to transcend these possible barriers, but the Holy Spirit does. You will encounter profound triumph and loss in these pages, which really is the story of all of our lives. May God Himself allow you to see yourself in these pages, even if your life story has played out under different circumstances than those of my own. God bless you, dear reader, and may you find my Jesus throughout these pages.

Praise be to the God and Father of our Lord Jesus Christ, the Father of compassion and the God of all comfort, who comforts us in all our troubles, so that we can comfort those in any trouble with the comfort we ourselves have received from God. For just as the sufferings of Christ flow over into our lives, so also through Christ our comfort overflows.   2 CORINTHIANS 1:3–5

Shawn Lantz
Nashville, Tennessee, 2008

Laban and Marcella Smith's wedding day, 1935.

Prologue

But from everlasting to everlasting the LORD's love is with those who fear him, and his righteousness with their children's children—with those who keep his covenant and remember to obey his precepts.　　　　—PSALM 103:17–18

In 1933, a successful young oral surgeon living in Grosse Pointe, Michigan, lost his wife, Ruby, to a brain tumor. Until this tragic circumstance occurred, Laban Smith seemed to have everything in life that one could wish for. Dr. Smith was a graduate of the University of Michigan Dental College with two thriving practices, an estate-sized home, and two precious children—a daughter, Phyllis, and a son, Herb. The thought had never occurred to him that his life could be missing anything, until his world was shattered by Ruby's death.

Distraught with grief, he decided to go to a small chapel on Gratiot Avenue, the busy thoroughfare on which one of his dental practices was located. A spinster lady preacher named Flossie Knopp shared the message of salvation through Jesus Christ with those attending the chapel service. The Holy Spirit spoke through Laban's fog of grief. He immediately realized he was lost and needed a Savior. Laban gave his broken heart to Christ that day, after realizing that Jesus was who he had been looking for all along. A later introduction of Laban Smith to Marcella Knopp, Flossie's younger sister, led to a proposal of marriage by

Smith family before the call to Congo. Left to right: Marcella, Laban, Herb, Phyllis.

Laban to Marcella after a whirlwind, two-month courtship in 1935.

Laban assumed that everyone would be as eager to accept God's gift of salvation through Christ as he had been. Not being able to keep his newfound joy to himself, Laban shared the gospel with every patient in his dental chair. The spring of 1938 found Laban restless as he shared with Marcella that he believed God was calling them to the Belgian Congo as missionaries.

Marcella initially balked at the idea of leaving everything and going to the African continent, mistaking Laban's certainty over God's call for new-believer exuberance. He persistently brought up the calling. Halfheartedly, Marcella typed a letter requesting acceptance of the Smiths as missionaries to the Belgian Congo. The letter was addressed to Unevangelized Tribes Mission (UTM). She took it to the post office, saying a prayer under her breath, "Lord, I've done my part; now You do Your part and make sure this letter gets lost!"

Smith family prayer card, 1938. Left to right: *Phyllis, Herb, Laban, Marcella.*

Five months after receiving the Lord's call to leave behind the successful life he had built for his family in the United States, Laban and Marcella sold everything and boarded the *Jean Jadot* ocean liner with Phyllis and Herb for the month-long voyage to the Congo.

So Begins
the Story...

Dr. Laban and Marcella Smith Congo-bound aboard the Jean Jadot, *October 20,
1938.*

Congo Vignettes

Stories of God's Faithfulness
to Three Generations in
the Heart of Africa

Chapter One

Power in the Blood

Ngolo Mu Menga Ya Yesu

"Lord, I have covenanted with You for 10,000 of these precious people. I thank You for the fire You have kindled in my heart; may it never go out." —an entry from Dr. Laban Smith's diary, written August 31, 1939

D o we believe the Lord hears the most obscure cries of hearts that are truly seeking Him? In the mid 1930s, a young oral surgeon with a thriving practice in Detroit, Michigan, had a dramatic encounter with Christ and was never the same again. Against all worldly wisdom, Dr. Laban Smith, my grandfather, sold his two dental practices and his large home in Grosse Pointe, Michigan. Along with his wife, Marcella, and two young children, he boarded the *Jean Jadot,* a ship bound for the Belgian Congo, in 1938. He had no formal Bible school training, had never been overseas, and had been a born-again believer in Christ for fewer than five years. But he knew God was calling, and he never looked back.

Upon their return to Congo in 1947, after an eighteen-month furlough in the United States, my grandparents felt the Lord was leading them to Iwungu, a new mission station in the province of Bandundu. This new post was several hundred miles away from the mission station of Kajiji, where they had previously ministered. During their nine years of ministry at Kajiji, the Lord had added two more children to the family, Jack and Jim. Unbeknownst to Laban and Marcella, a chief of the Bayanzi people from the village of Longo, was visited in prison by men who had received salvation under the ministry of my grandparents. Chief Kuma-Kuma ("Coo-ma-Coo-ma") was so intrigued by the story of the gospel that, although he had not yet made a personal decision for salvation in Christ, he sent men from his village to ask Dr. Smith to come and tell his people about who Jesus Christ was and what He had done for them.

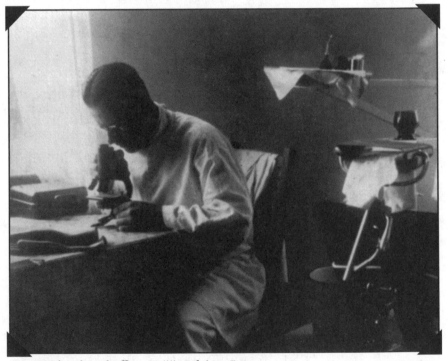

Dr. Smith's dental office, Kajiji, Belgian Congo.

Six weeks after being visited by the men of the village of Longo and another village, Nkara, Dr. Smith loaded up the International Panel truck and made the sixty-five-mile trip from Iwungu to these villages. National pastors and an evangelist named Toma accompanied my grandfather. Dr.

Smith spoke several times that first day, going first to the village of Longo and then to the village of Nkara, the father and mother villages of the Bayanzi people. The Bayanzi had been practicing child sacrifice to try to atone for their sins. After hearing and understanding that God the Father had sacrificed His perfect Son, Jesus Christ, to atone for their sins, they readily accepted God's gift of salvation through His Son. The Bayanzi joyfully realized that it was now unnecessary for their own children to be sacrificed.

Word spread quickly. Other villages cried out for Dr. Smith and the team to come to them, and for six weeks, Dr. Smith traveled to well over fifty villages. One of the outward signs of a true conversion was the burning of fetishes. Fetishes consisted of a large squash, dried and cut in half and filled with dirt, goat manure, and an antelope horn with a red parrot feather in the mixture. This filth is what they worshiped. Usually the fetish was kept under the father's bed. But now, instead of filth, Jesus Christ, the holy Son of God, became the focus of their grateful worship. The fetishes were burned. Before the life-changing power of the gospel came to the Bayanzi, the destruction of the fetishes was unthinkable. This was because the belief had been passed down from generation to generation for centuries that they were never to burn the "heirlooms" from their ancestors. The blood of Jesus Christ crushed the power of Satan. Chains of fear and ignorance caused by sin were now broken; captives were set free. Thousands of Bayanzi responded to the gospel and received the forgiveness offered by the blood of Jesus Christ.

The Belgian government could not understand the intensity of excitement among the Bayanzi relating to their recent conversion to Christ. The officials felt it was a temporary, emotional phenomenon. They asked Dr. Smith and the national pastors not to baptize anyone for a period of two years. The Belgian officials informed my grandfather that, "After two years, Dr. Smith, you will see that very few of them will be interested in whatever this 'being born again' is all about. We ask you to wait to baptize these people until two years have passed." In order to show the power of the blood of Christ to bring about permanent change in the lives of those who would believe the message of the gospel, my grandfather complied with the government's wishes and did not baptize anyone for two years.

Smith family at Kajiji, 1942. Left to right standing: *Jack, Laban, Phyllis, Herb, Marcella* (sitting holding baby Jim).

In 1949, two years after the phenomenal response of the Bayanzi to the gospel message, the first of four major baptismal services took place at the lake on the new mission station of Nkara-Ewa. The Bayanzi people had avoided the lake because of the belief that evil spirits hovered over its

Dr. Smith baptizing Congolese national in the Ntsianguna River during the Bayanzi awakening, 1949.

waters. The village of Mpene had fought the village of Longo over ownership of the village of Nkara and the fallen warriors' corpses had been dumped in the lake. My father, Jim, remembers sitting in a small boat on the lake as a seven-year-old boy during one of those services. He watched that day as twelve hundred people waited to give testimony to the fact that the blood of Jesus and His peace had freed them from the terror they had known under the power of the spirits of their ancestors. Seven pastors and my grandfather waded into Lake Ewa's waters to baptize these people in the name of the Father, Son, and Holy Spirit. Among those being baptized were many who had once participated in cannibalism, witchcraft, and child sacrifice. My grandfather had the foresight to record one of these momentous baptismal services on a 78-rpm record, which has survived the years. By 1952, five years after the initial invitation by the villages of Longo and Nkara, my grandfather's request of the Lord thirteen years earlier for the salvation of ten thousand precious Congolese people had been answered.

Is there power in the blood of Christ? Fast-forward fifty-six years to 2008. Two generations have passed since then. The rival villages of Longo and Nkara-Ewa are at peace. Nkara-Ewa, once a place of death, cannibalism, and child sacrifice, has been transformed into a life-giving center. Now on the hill overlooking the lake that was once a grave-yard of dead men's bones stands Laban Bible Institute, which has graduated more than five hundred men and women who continue telling the story of the transforming power of the blood of Jesus Christ.

Chapter Two

Be Still My Soul

Pemisa Ntima

Congo had two seasons: the rainy season and the dry season. During the rainy season, the daytime temperature would reach a sweltering 100-plus degrees Fahrenheit, and we would be able to see the beginnings of a thunderstorm roll in across the lake where we played as children. These storms would often happen at night, which was mesmerizing to watch. As the lightning split the sky and illuminated trees being blown and tossed by the howling wind, Nicol, Todd, and I would

The beautiful Lake Ewa in front of our childhood home.

often gather with our parents on our three-sided screened upstairs porch to watch the storm whip up the waters of the lake.

I usually looked forward to the thunder and lightning these storms produced until one night when Dad wasn't home. He had gone on an evangelism trip with a team of men around dusk earlier in the evening. It had been an intensely hot day—a day in which I felt as if my skin were melting from the heat. I remember seeing a bolt of lightning followed by a thunderclap that almost caused me to scream because of its deafening volume. That night, as I lay on my bed in the dark, I was suddenly aware of a new, unsettling emotion. Fear in my heart gripped me as I heard the moan of the wind rise in pitch. It sounded ominous and threatening. I listened to the storm in my bed for several more seconds as my twelve-year-old mind envisioned the wind and the storm as a monster seeking to devour me. I ran into my parents' room and screamed my mother's name. I felt some relief as she responded, but I really wanted my dad. If Dad was there I knew I would be all right, but he wasn't with me that night. He was riding out the storm on the grasslands somewhere, completely inaccessible to me.

Although the thunder and wind together produced a cacophony of dreadful noise, Nicol, Todd, and even my baby brother, Jack, slept through the storm. Every now and then I would call out to my mother to see if she was awake and as aware of the storm as I was. I decided my parents' room was the safest one in which to hide during the storm. The tempest outside was the most violent one I could remember. I will never forget the tremendous terror I felt as I listened to the horrible symphony of cymbal-like crashes that sounded when part of the tin roof blew off our house that night. I wanted my dad. I knew the storm would not

Smith family picture, 1981. Left to right: *Jack, Shawn, Nancy, Jim, Todd, Nicol* (holding pet monkey, T.D.)

have been as terrifying to me if I knew that he was with me in the darkness.

As a child, I only had to be aware of my father's presence or absence in the house to determine how I would face the storm. My bedroom was only feet away from my parents' room, and knowing my dad was there during the storm made thunder and lightning a terrifying delight to my twelve-year-old mind. I sensed the danger of the storm, but knowing my daddy was present allowed me to be aware of the danger without the fear of harm. In his absence, the same thunder and lightning caused intense fright as well as feelings of isolation.

Being an adult has robbed me of my ability as a child to be calmed by another human being's presence during the thunder of my circumstances. The childlike faith I had in my father's strength at age twelve allowed me to view the storm with delight as the lightning flashed and the thunder rolled, knowing I could watch safely at a distance, knowing I was under his protection. I have come to realize how I will weather the storms in my adult life is dependent upon my ability to exercise the same childlike faith in my heavenly Father's protection as I had in my father's ability to save me from harm.

Would I realize my desperate need for Christ's presence in my life without the storms? I have lived enough of life to know the answer to that question is a resounding no. When life is going along with no thunder rumbling ominously behind me, how easily I forget where my security lies. Without the storm, I am too often trusting in created things rather than my Creator. The storm makes me see the truth I find in Psalm 81:7 (AMP):

"You called in distress and I delivered you; I answered you in the secret place of thunder . . ."

My ears, once so busy listening to the many distractions of life before the storm, are now able to hear Christ's voice in a way I was not able to hear during my days of ease and sunshine. A profound truth has been my realization of this paradox: It is when my world is most in turmoil and I have called out to Him to rescue me in the middle of the raging wind that I have heard Him in the secret place of my thunder. Only after I have acknowledged my state of helplessness and fear am I able to recapture that twelve-year-old child's ability to trust that my God is with me in the midst of the lightning and thunderstorms of life. I can watch the tempest safely, unshaken by the terror that cannot stand when my soul is still in His presence. I am safe in my heavenly Father's protection.

Be still my soul:
The waves and winds still know,
His voice who ruled them
While He dwelt below.
　　　—KATHERINA AMALIA VON SCHLEGEL
　　　(1697–?) Translated into English by
　　　Jane Laurie Borthwick (1813–1897)

Chapter Three

Great Is Thy Faithfulness

Kwikama Nene, Kieleka Nene

November 14, 1978

"Dear Diary,
Guess what my mom told me, Nicol, and Todd tonight?!
That she is going to have a baby! It's going to be born in June.
I am so excited!"   —Entry from my diary at age ten

Just three weeks before our departure date of December 6, 1978, to the Democratic Republic of Congo (formerly known as Zaire under President Mobutu Sese Seko), my mother gave us the wonderful news she was expecting a baby. The baby would be born on the African continent we would soon call home. As children, we were blissfully ignorant at how frightening the prospect of childbirth was in a foreign country to my mother. She would be six hours away from the nearest hospital, with no telephone and no doctor nearby should the pregnancy develop complications. Anxious thoughts filled her mind regarding the conditions in which she might find herself bringing this new child into the world. Nicol, Todd, and I only knew our request over the years for another sibling had been fulfilled.

"Daddy, are we there yet?" Left to right: Nicol, Shawn, Todd *during our first flight to Congo, 1978.*

Our dad had talked to us about the new home that we would be living in and how our new playmates would speak a different language than we did. He told us about the twenty-acre lake in our front yard in which he had played as a boy to escape the intense heat of the Congo sun. We were excited at the thought of living on the same mission station in which he had lived in and experiencing the places of his childhood.

Three months after our arrival in the Congo, we were all in the throes of culture shock, learning the difficult lesson that what we imagined was not living up to our expectations. Our new life was devoid of modern conveniences that we children had taken for granted in the United States. Nicol's and my favorite television show was *Little House on the Prairie.* We had romanticized the pioneer life and had pretended we were Laura Ingalls many times in our play. Now we found ourselves right in the middle of those late nineteenth-century conditions with no running water, television, or telephone access. We had limited electricity. As the loneliness of being the only American family on our bush mission station set in, we longed for the ability to quit "playing" pioneer life and go back to the life we once knew. Mail could take up to six months to reach us. We desperately missed our Grandpa and Grandma McKown, Uncle Paul, Aunt Gerry, and our cousins, Terri and Mark.

To pass the long days, Nicol and I would ask Mom to unpack the baby's suitcase of clothing so that we could exclaim in wondering delight over how small our new baby brother or sister would be and smell the baby powder. We would talk about how much we loved him or her already. The conversation would always end with the same question asked of us to our mother: "How much longer, Mom, until the baby is born?" The time of waiting seemed endless to us.

On June 28, 1979, our healthy baby brother, John Scott Smith, was born on the same mission station in which our grandmother had given birth to our father thirty-seven years earlier. The grace of God had seen my mother through her fears regarding Jack's birth. Although I know that many siblings anticipate the birth of a new baby, I was sure that no baby was more wanted and loved than my baby brother, Jack, my Uncle Jack's namesake. Taking care of him and his needs became a joy to my mother, sister, and me. Jack's birth gave us a purpose during the monotonous days before we felt acclimated to our new culture. Nicol, Todd, and I would have contests to see who could make him laugh or smile the most. From his earliest days, we wanted Jack with us constantly and would run to pick him up at his slightest whimper.

By the time Jack was nine months old, we had been living at Nkara-Ewa for one year. My parents had agreed

Shawn and her real-life baby doll, Jack, 1980.

that the time had come for my father to leave the mission station for an extended period of time. A recently purchased short-wave radio now allowed us to communicate with the nearest missionary doctor five hours away. The week-long evangelism trip with the seven Bible school students would give my father and the men their first joint opportunity to share Christ with surrounding villages. This was the first time my mother would be left alone on the mission station with her children. The airstrip was being built at the time, but was not yet ready for the MAF (Mission Aviation Fellowship) planes to land on it. Mom stood outside our home watching the truck disappear up the quarter-mile drive to the top of the hill. She knew that if anything happened to us while he was gone, she would have no way of communicating with him, and no airplane could fly in if there was a medical emergency. The situation called for a large leap of faith in God's protection on her part. In her mind's eye, she saw a week of isolation because she could not yet communicate in the trade language of Kituba.

Within an hour of Dad's departure, Jack started vomiting. A feeling of dread came over Mom, but with Jack being her fourth child, panic did not immediately set in. Perhaps Jack just had a twenty-four-hour flu and would be better in the morning. With the onset of Jack's diarrhea, however, Mom became more alarmed. Jack's vomiting and diarrhea continued all through the dark, sleepless hours of the night. In the morning, Mom called the doctor on the short-wave radio for advice. By this time, Jack was not able to keep anything in his stomach. The doctor told her to continue giving him fluids, including sugary Coca-Cola, to keep him hydrated.

Jack listlessly clung to Mom. The only time she put him down was to change his cloth diapers. Limited quantities of diapers and line-drying forced Mom to resort to using pillowcases, towels, and even bed sheets as day two turned into day three and day three eventually turned into day five. Mom had never known the fear that came from the helplessness of having only one radio contact each night at six-thirty. Dehydration was becoming a real possibility. A desperation she had not yet experienced came over her. God had to intervene. My terrified mother, who felt like a stranger in an alien land, begged God to act on her baby's behalf.

Mom summoned Nicol, Todd, and me into her bedroom. We had been unaware of how serious Jack's condition had been. I was eleven years old, Nicol was nine, and Todd was six. Our ages made us unable to offer any real advice or support to my mother during this time. We were shocked at the depth of her distress.

Day five of Jack's illness fell on a Sunday. We could hear the joyful worship music coming from the unscreened church windows in the valley. Mom told us she wanted us to go with her to the church building to have the church pray over Jack. In the year of living on the mission station, we had picked up the Kituba language quite easily. For Mom, however, learning the language had been a most frustrating and slow process. She needed us to communicate to the Congolese worshipers how serious Jack's illness was and to ask for prayer.

Jack was wrapped in a bed sheet and carried in my mother's arms as we made our way down to the church from our house. Tears were streaming down our faces as we begged God to save our little brother. My mother had tried everything she knew to do for Jack. The only thing now that would save his life was the healing hand of God Himself.

The stone church building had been planned by our grandfather, Laban, and built by our grandmother, Marcella, after his death. No expensive carpeting, cherry-wood padded pews, or decorations adorned the inside of the building. It had only a simple cement floor, which had cracked in many places in the twenty-five years since it had been built. Rough-hewn benches with no backs were lined up in two sections facing a simple cement platform which contained a wooden pulpit.

Our skin color made us the object of everyone's attention anywhere we went. Every eye in the building was on us as we entered a side door of the church. The service immediately went on hold as loud whispers were exchanged among the worshipers, who were trying to guess why my mother was crying as she held Jack. I don't recall which one of us children related to the pastor the reason for our sudden appearance, but I do remember a group of men circling us as they each laid a hand on Jack or on one of us. I knew then, as an eleven-year-old girl, that there is no unknown language that goes before the throne of God. The Holy Spirit was in the middle of our small group that morning in the Bandundu Province in the bush of Africa.

The Congolese are some of the poorest people materially on the earth, with the average family making only one hundred U.S. dollars per year in buying power. However, God has blessed them with an astounding amount of faith. James 2:5 says: "Listen, dear brothers: Has not God chosen those who are poor in the eyes of the world to be rich in faith and to inherit the kingdom He promised those who love Him?" In an effort to show my mother their deep concern for our family, an unsolicited all-night prayer meeting was held by the Congolese for our brother.

My mother woke with a start on Monday morning with the realization that Jack had not vomited all night. As she reached out to hold her now peaceful, happy baby in her arms, she knew that her heavenly Father had held her in the palm of His hand. My mom's worst fear had come to pass while my father was gone. Her baby had become deathly ill. God had shown her, through her terror, that she had never been alone. As promised, He had been her rearguard and had orchestrated every detail.

For when You did awesome things that we did not expect, You came down, and the mountains trembled before You. Since ancient times no one has heard, no ear has perceived, no eye has seen any God besides You, who acts on behalf of those who wait for Him. —ISAIAH 64:3–4

My mother dreaded being left alone that week. She had no way of knowing that Jack's illness would allow the mountain of fear in her heart to tremble before the Lord who came down Himself to heal her baby. She was able to see the Lord act on her behalf as she threw herself on His mercy and waited for Him to rescue her. He showed her she did not need a hospital or a doctor. He was the great Physician who delighted in showing her His faithfulness.

Jack marries Molly Styer, July 7, 2000.

Chapter Four

His Eye Is on the Sparrow

Ndeke Fioti Nzambi Ke Tala

Are not two sparrows sold for a penny? Yet not one of these will fall to the ground apart from the will of Your Father. And even the very hairs of your head are all numbered. So don't be afraid; you are worth more than many sparrows.
—Matthew 10:29–31

It was November 10, 1977, and winter had come early to our part of western Michigan. Frost and snow were predicted that night and our mother had learned from the previous winter that our home's poorly insulated water pipes froze quickly. Our only alternative for water was the artesian well in the back of the house. Dad was away in California at meetings, singing as a music evangelist. Trying to avoid the unpleasant experience of trekking outside in the frigid air to dip her bucket repeatedly for water, my mother decided to light the family room oil space heater. Her hope was that the heater's warmth would prevent the pipes from freezing. Nicol, Todd, and I settled down in front of the television on our parents' king-sized bed to watch *The Waltons*. About ten minutes later, Mom smelled the odor of a searing iron. She walked from the bedroom through the living room and into the kitchen, where, to her horror, she saw the entire family room wall engulfed in flames.

Before we became missionaries, 1976. Left to right: Jim, Todd, Nancy, Shawn, Nicol.

We lived sixteen miles outside of the town of New Era, Michigan. Our home was situated in the country, far away from the nearest fire station. My mother's screams urged us to get out of the house and run to our grandmother's trailer, located three hundred feet away from our house on our ten acres of property. Nicol and Todd quickly obeyed, but in my concern for her safety, I refused to leave my mother until we left the house together. I remember my mom picking up the phone to call the fire department. She found out some time later that two fire departments argued over whose township was responsible for going to the house.

The fire's roar was growing louder as my mother hung up the phone. "Shawnee, we have to get out right now." I could hear the strain in her voice. She and I ran for the front porch, the farthest exit away from the fire's origin. As our feet hit the ground, we heard the windows burst, the floor collapse, and the furnace explode.

I can remember how small my voice sounded as I screamed, "Help, help, fire!" over and over again until I was hoarse. The black frigid night seemed to swallow the sound. My mother and I parted ways in the front driveway. She instructed me to meet up with Nicol and Todd at my grandmother's trailer. The walk required me to pass the burning house. I watched with a horrified fascination as the flames licked up the wooden clapboards. Even though I was only nine, I knew help would not get there in time to save our seventy-three-year-old farmhouse.

My mother, clad in her nightgown and an old bed-spread, ran barefooted down the gravel driveway, continuing an eighth of a mile across the street to our nearest neighbors' house, screaming "Fire!" all the way. There was nothing anyone could do to save the house. It vanished before her eyes in twenty minutes, destroying fourteen years of married and family life she had built with our dad. The unquenchable flames greedily consumed the irreplaceable history of our family documented in pictures and home movies, and sixteen-millimeter film from Dr. Laban and Marcella Smith's ministry in the Congo. In the middle of the awful trauma of watching her life's treasures disintegrate before her eyes, Jesus tenderly spoke to her heart with His own words found in Matthew 6:19–21: "Do not store up for yourselves treasures on earth where moth and rust destroy . . . But store up for yourselves treasures in heaven . . . For where your treasure is, there will your heart be also."

Was the Lord there that night as the fire took away every material possession our family had? Was He aware of

The Smith Family singers, minus Dad, 1978. Left to right: *Nicol, Shawn, Nancy, Todd.*

what was going on? Does He check out when our dreams lie shattered and smoldering around us? If not a sparrow falls apart from His will and the very hairs of our head are numbered, then we must believe there are no surprises to Him. We could not have known that November night that losing our home would set in motion a chain of events leading to our family being called to the Congo. The very sorrow that caused such grief would enable us to obtain eternal treasures that moth and thieves and yes, even fire, would never destroy. We arrived in the Congo, then known as Zaire, one year and three weeks after the fire.

King David, who God called a man after His own heart, penned these words under the inspiration of the Holy Spirit in 2 Samuel 22:29–33:

> *You are my lamp, O LORD; the LORD turns my darkness into light. With Your help I can advance against a troop; with my God I can scale a wall. As for God His way is perfect; the Word of the Lord is flawless. He is a shield for all who take refuge in him. For who is God besides the LORD? And who is the Rock except our God? It is God who arms me with strength and makes my way perfect.*

Even when my soul is sitting in darkness and fear, the Lord has the ability to bring light to me there. He promises that His way is perfect, His Word is flawless, and that He is a shield for all who take refuge in Him. He also is the One who arms me with strength and makes my way perfect. Without God's perspective, the fire we experienced that cold November night in 1977 could easily have been considered a tragedy. Catastrophes like this may cause bitterness and feelings of abandonment, and, yes, even feelings of disappointment and anger toward God. God's Word is truth. Believing, in spite of our circumstances, that He cannot lie or be unfaithful to us allows us to see Him turn our would-be tragedy into triumph.

What is tragedy? I have had to redefine my previous definition of the word. Tragedy is carrying around the burden of trying to find one's self-worth and value in earthly treasures that can be here today and gone tomorrow. Tragedy is continuing to be enslaved to the gnawing fear that we control our own destinies and there is no larger plan or purpose for our lives than what we are currently living. Tragedy is never having a real-life experience that forces us to have to throw ourselves on the mercy of the One who created us. In trusting God with our circumstances, no matter how dire they may be, we prepare the way for Him to rescue us so we may praise Him for those very circumstances. Tragedy is not believing God can use our pain for His glory and, instead, believing He has abandoned us.

When our lives are pierced with pain and sorrow, we can rest in the knowledge of the simple, but profound truth found in Matthew's gospel: The God who sees every sparrow fall from the sky watches over us with a Father's heart.

Chapter Five

I Need Thee Every Hour

Konso Ntangu Ke Nfunu

t was a stifling Saturday with a searing sun in the sky, but the students of Ubangi Academy were oblivious to the heat as we piled, screaming with delight, into the back of the large pickup truck that would take us to beautiful Lake Kwada. Everyone looked forward to these special times when our dorm parents would declare an afternoon of fun in its cool waters some distance away from our school campus. Our Saturday morning chores had been done, and now all students, from the youngest second grader to the towering senior boys, were exhilarated at the thought of the water games and supper out at the lake. My fellow female seventh-grade classmates and I giggled and whispered together as we planned what our day would involve.

Everyone had settled into the almost hour-long journey when the pickup, with no prior warning, suddenly sputtered and died. All of us MKs (missionary kids) were familiar enough with this occurrence to merely groan, but not panic. Bush living had conditioned us to know there was no roadside assistance available to take us to our destination, no service stations, and no land phones in that part of the country. Our only option was to walk. It was decided that two older boys would head back to the mission station of

Karawa to get another vehicle to transport us all back. If the boys were disappointed at this change of plans from being at the lake to spending the majority of their afternoon walking back to school, they did not show it at all. They promptly set off back down the road. The rest of the students, with our dorm parents, started the forty-five-minute walk in the opposite direction to Lake Kwada. The sun was blazing in the sky that early afternoon and my freckled skin turned a deep pink under the brown spots. We sang songs to pass the time and were finally rewarded with the sight of the lake through the trees.

We all sprinted toward the lake, dropping our towels and stepping out of our shoes. Most of the afternoon was spent in the water, which was deliciously cool after our hot jaunt down the dirt road where we had left our disabled vehicle. Around suppertime, I started feeling out of sorts. Although the sun had been merciless in its intensity, I developed chills that belied the weather. I decided to leave my friends in the water and lie down in the small home that missionary families used for vacations at the lake. *Maybe I need a nap,* I thought, hoping against hope I would recover enough to enjoy the rest of the day. One of my dorm mothers, Aunt Joyce Falconer, came to see how I was faring and to offer me a plate of supper. I miserably told her I had no appetite.

The "big boys"—as we "little kids" referred to them— returned sometime after supper with another vehicle to take us all home. I can remember feeling only half aware as my schoolmates piled into the back of the truck, screaming and laughing. I was helped into the front cab of the vehicle to lay my head on the lap of Aunt Joyce, who stroked my forehead and tried to comfort me with promises of my bed and a good rest, which would probably take care of my chills and nausea. That is the last thing I clearly remember about

Smiths on furlough, 1982–83. Left to right (standing): *Nicol, Todd, Shawn.* Left to right (sitting): *Jim, Jack, Nancy.*

that day or the next several, as delirium set in from the sun-stroke that was the result of the walk in the midday Congo sun.

Although I was not lucid many of the days I was so violently ill, a memory that stands out very starkly in my mind was the thought that I wanted my mom. I was very aware of her absence. During moments I was cognizant of my surroundings, I was terrified at the thought that I was alone without her to care for me, as only she could. My roommate had been moved to another room during my illness. I must have called out enough for my mother be-cause those looking over me requested the mother of the Colby girls to move into my room to be there when I woke up to ask for water or my mother. The few times I do remember waking up, I recall Aunt Norma sitting in a chair next to my bed while talking to me and trying to comfort me. She cheerfully and tenderly acted as surrogate mother during those confusing, dark days of my convalescence. I could not do anything for myself, and she would help me find my way to the bathroom, put cold compresses on my feverish forehead, or clean up after me.

Although my dorm parents had been deeply concerned for my welfare, it was decided that my parents would not be informed of the illness until the worst part of it had passed. I have full assurance the Lord directed them to tell my parents about my illness only after I was on the road to recovery.

When I flew home for my next school break, my mother and I cried together about that time of being apart. Having three children of my own, I can see the situation with a mother's heart, and I realize my mother's tears of sorrow were over her ignorance of my illness and her inability to comfort me. My twelve-year-old tears reminded me how greatly I missed her comfort. It was not until years later, while reading Psalm 139, that the Lord let me see the truth of His presence even when I missed my own mother so intensely.

> *Where can I go from Your Spirit? Where can I flee from your presence? If I go up to the heavens, you are there; if I make my bed in the depths, you are there. If I rise on the wings of the dawn, if I settle on the far side of the sea, even there your hand will guide me, your right hand will hold me fast. If I say, "Surely the darkness will hide me and the light become night around me," even the darkness will not be dark to you; the night will shine like the day, for darkness is as light to you.*
>
> —PSALM 139:7–12

Because my world was so literal at twelve years old, I rarely had the ability to sense the Lord's presence. Comfort to me at that age meant my mother's voice and touch. Things that were tangible and that were in my line of vision constituted what was real to me. Because she was not there, I could not feel truly comforted. I lacked the capacity to see beyond what my human eyes had in their sight.

Shawn marries Rob Lantz, June 19,1993.

I have come to see that this lack of vision is the result of my condition as a fallible human being without the capacity to explain painful experiences to my satisfaction. Only after asking God to give me spiritual eyes have I begun to be content with not having all the reasons why He has allowed me to experience trials. I do not have all the answers. I have come to this ironic conclusion: I do not need to have all the questions answered as long as I am assured of His presence. The peace that comes with letting go of needing concrete answers from Him to my deepest hurts has grown in proportion to my willingness to acknowledge my desperate need for Him. It is then that I can see His presence when I look back on my darkest hours.

Regardless of where I am, what my circumstances are, or whether or not I see the Lord immediately in my situation, He promises me that He busies Himself with my every step. My darkness is not darkness to Him at all; on the contrary, my darkness shines as clear as day to Him. If life takes me to the exhilarating mountaintop in my soul or to the depths of despair, pain, depression, or grief, He is thoroughly acquainted with all my ways and profoundly cares about my situation even more than I do. He holds me fast with His right hand and will never let me go.

> I need Thee every hour, in joy or pain;
> Come quickly and abide, or life is vain!
> I need Thee, O I need Thee; Every hour I need Thee;
> O bless me now, my Savior: I come to Thee.
> —ANNIE SHERWOOD HAWKS (1835–1918)

Chapter Six

We'll Understand It Better By and By

Beto Bakisa Yo Mbote Bye n Bye

Laban and Marcella were reflecting on God's faithfulness during their fifteen-year missionary career in the Belgian Congo. Although they had buried baby Gareth in the United States on furlough in 1946, the Lord had seen Marcella through the births of two healthy sons in 1939 and 1942. Ten thousand Bayanzi people had come to know Christ in a period of five years. God had supplied every physical need and had protected the family from major illnesses. Reflection awakened gratefulness in both of them over God's bountiful blessings in the ministry He had given them among His people.

On the morning of January 24, 1953, Dr. Smith went to look at the new home he was building on the mission station of Nkara-Ewa. The rafters on the upper-story roof had to be nailed securely before the tin roof could go on. The home was beautiful. The stone had been quarried from the other side of the hill on the mission station. Beautiful rose- and blue-colored streaks ran through the stone. Because of the intense heat of the rainy season, two screened porches, one on each level of the home, had been constructed to allow cross ventilation in order to cool the home. The structure was near completion.

Dr. Laban H. Smith (1898–1953).

Dr. Smith climbed the ladder and started to pound nails into the piece of lumber he was leaning over. A brilliant Congolese mason named Toma was working with him on the house. Laban needed to move his foot to secure a more stable position on the rafter, but having just recovered from mild sunstroke and a case of malaria, he misjudged his movement and crashed to the cement floor eight feet below. Toma's screams brought my grandmother and Congolese running to Dr. Smith's side.

Nkara-Ewa was nine hours away from the nearest hospital in the city of Kikwit. The roads were unpredictable—either full of mud from the rains or possibly impassable from the sand of the dry season. Marcella numbly gathered Jack and Jim to her side and asked thirteen-year-old Jack to start the truck. Ten-year-old Jim climbed in beside him on the front seat. The Congolese helped her to load Laban in the truck. *Dear God! This must be a nightmare; I surely will wake up soon! This cannot be Your perfect plan . . .* , she thought. Marcella and a friend sat on either side of Laban during the arduous journey to the hospital, throughout which Dr. Smith never regained consciousness. One hour after arriving in Kikwit, Dr. Smith walked through the gates of eternity to hear his Master say, "Well done, my good and faithful servant. Enjoy your rest."

Two days after Laban Smith had been buried in the soil of Congo among the people God had enabled him to love so completely, my grandmother, Marcella, captured her initial feelings and actions in a letter to her family upon hearing from the doctor that her husband had gone on to be with the Lord:

> *I knelt beside the chair in the hospital and asked God for strength to bear the weight that had been thrust upon me. He is sustaining, but through the days, I will need Him more . . . I had been preparing the boys when I saw there was no hope and told them Daddy would be going. They said, "Going where?" I said, "To be with Jesus, if the Lord does not undertake." Finally, it began to dawn on them. They took it well because that living*

hope is bright within their hearts. But now I must find the answers for their questions. Jimmie said this morning, "If I pray to God, will He let Daddy talk to me? What clothing will he wear?" I said, "Jim, the King's children are all glorious within (Psalm 45). There is a portion [of Scripture] that says the saints are clothed in light. And whatever it is it will be wonderful."

Scripture tells us that those of us who have accepted Christ as our Savior are children of the King of glory. I believe Laban was dressed in clothes suited for a prince because it was his coronation day. He was ushered into the very presence of the Most High King the moment his earthly life ended. It is why those of us who have made Christ our King do not grieve as those with no hope.

Marcella Smith and Nancy Smith at gravesite of Dr. Laban Smith in Kikwit Cemetery, Congo, 1969.

I never had the privilege of knowing this man who loved his God so fervently. However, I see the legacy my grandfather, Laban, left that day in 1953. I have seen him in the life of my father, Jim, who is possibly even more of a visionary than Dr. Smith. I am a recipient of the blessing of his and my grandmother's prayers for grandchildren he would never live to see.

> *I tell you the truth, unless a kernel of wheat falls to the ground and dies, it remains only a single seed. But if it dies, it produces many seeds. The man who loves his life will lose it, while the man who hates his life in this world will keep it for eternal life. Whoever serves me must follow me; and where I am my servant also will be. My Father will honor the one who serves me.*
>
> —JOHN 12:24–27

A human mind cannot comprehend why Laban Smith would die during the height of his ministry. Scripture reveals the truth that every day of our lives is ordained by God, before the first day begins. The day of our death is also known. From that perspective, my grandfather's life was full and complete because there are no surprises to the One who calls Himself "I AM." Jesus has been faithful to His promise in John 12. I have personally met many of the seeds that Laban Smith's life and death produced in the lives of the Congolese he died serving. First Corinthians 13:12 provides insight into the questions that are left unanswered in this life: "Now we see but a poor reflection as in a mirror; then we shall see face-to-face. Now I know in part; then I shall know fully, even as I am fully known."

We will understand it better by and by.

Chapter Seven

God Gave Us Our Hands

Nzambi Pesaka Beto Maboko Ya Beto

I was getting ready for bed at my Grandma McKown's house the evening of March 2, 1973. Before I lay down on my small pallet of blankets next to her bed, I told her I needed to pray for my new little brother. The reason I was staying overnight was because my mother had gone to the hospital in labor earlier that afternoon.

"How do you know that the baby is a boy?" she asked.

"Because Jesus told me he was going to be a boy," I replied simply. Grandma came closer to hear the short prayer from my five-year-old lips and tucked me in. I was not surprised the following morning when she told me my brother, James Todd Smith, had arrived a few hours after I had gone to sleep.

Todd quickly distinguished himself as the only boy in our family. His lack of shyness was apparent when he decided he was going to preach at the age of three. He would dress himself in his suit, complete with a bowtie, and call his congregation—which consisted of our mother, Grandma Marcella, Nicol, and me—to listen to his fiery expositions. Todd was confident he could preach along with the best of them, but he told my mother, "Mama, I hope Calvary Baptist [our home church in Michigan] doesn't want me to preach to them when we visit." He had no fear of the large pulpit or the two-thousand-seat auditorium; he simply was not interested in providing the sermon that day.

Todd always had a tender heart. My mother was in the kitchen one day overhearing a conversation Todd was having out loud with himself. "Jesus," five-year-old Todd asked, "if I open my mouth really big, will You come into my heart?" Believing he was the man of the family while

Todd and his best boyhood friend, Narro, with a bird they had hunted, 1981.

Dad was away on the road singing, Todd would often sleep on Dad's side of the bed to offer Mom the protection his little-boy mind believed she needed.

One of these nights, Mom was crying softly because of a stressful circumstance. Not realizing Todd was awake beside her, she was surprised when his little voice came out of the darkness to ask her why she was crying. Mom tried to swallow her tears and gave a vague explanation that she was sad about something that had happened.

"But, Mama, I love you with all of my heart!" To Todd, his wholehearted devotion to my mother was enough for any sadness to be erased on her part.

Todd also had a practical side. The spring before our house fire, Todd had helped Mom scrape off the chipping white paint on our farmhouse in Hesperia. As the house burned to the ground, Todd found his way to my mother's side.

"Well, Mama," he said, "at least we won't have to worry about painting it next summer!" My mother smiled through her tears as she embraced him.

Thirteen months after the fire, our family had arrived in the Congo. My parents had told us we were going to live in Congo for three and a half years before we would return to the United States for furlough. After enduring three days of stifling heat, unfamiliar foods, and itching his numerous mosquito bites, Todd said, "Okay, we have stayed in Africa for three days now. We've been here long *enough!* I'm sick of this place—it's too hot. Let's go back to America!"

Nicol and I capitalized on Todd's trusting heart. Never thinking we would purposefully keep vital information from him, Todd's gullibility made him the target of more than one of our pranks. We knew we could get him to do almost anything if chocolate was the promised reward. Sweets were a very hard treat to come by in the bush. I don't remember if the mastermind behind the bouillon-cube prank was Nicol or me, but we soon had Todd convinced chocolate was in the middle of the cube. Poor Todd became more distressed while sucking on the cube we had promised him contained chocolate in its middle.

"I just taste yucky flavor and salt," he informed us.

Nicol and I made a poor attempt at concealing our laughter.

"Are you guys tricking me?" he finally asked. We assured him that we were not tricking him, and suggested he bite into the cube to get to its middle more quickly. He did so and took off after us with flailing fists as he realized our deception.

One day Dad suggested we go to a new place he called "Mystery Point" over East Hill on the station. The hill loomed large to our young eyes, but we all gamely went with Dad one afternoon. Todd was full of energy and excitement as we climbed the hill. Along the trip up East Hill, his enthusiasm spilled over as he informed Nicol and me of his excitement that Cedar Point was right over the hill. We had visited the Ohio amusement park, Cedar Point, several times before we moved to Congo. All of us had been enthralled by the rides and relived our experiences at the park many times in conversation. Todd had mistakenly thought Dad had said, "Cedar Point" instead of "Mystery Point." Nicol and I, being three and five years older respectively, decided not to correct Todd's mistaken belief that the park was so close to us. We played right along with him. Todd couldn't wait to get to the top. After an hour of climbing and walking the summit for a while, his excitement turned to disgust. The other side of the hill, Todd quickly realized, was just the other side of the hill! "Where are all those rides and roller coasters? I thought we were going to Cedar Point!" Todd demanded to know. Dad had to explain we were more than eight thousand miles away from Ohio. Todd could not understand why that distance was an impediment to our present situation.

While swimming in the lake one afternoon, Nicol and I started shouting out nonsensical phrases and realized that the hills surrounding the lake would bounce the sound back to us. The two of us got Todd's attention the next time his head came up from under the water.

"Hey, Todd, listen to this. When I say something, 'Echo' will repeat what I say back," I told him.

"Who's 'Echo'?" Todd wanted to know.

"Oh," I replied, "he's this person who never says anything by himself. He just repeats what everyone else says. He's a copycat."

I could see the doubt about the truth of my story in my brother's eyes. Nicol, however, quickly confirmed everything I had said. We spent much of the next hour shouting out phrases that bounced back to our ears. Todd was a true believer of our tall tale by the time we walked back up the hill to the house.

Several days had passed since the deception. I did not know that Todd had been thinking about "Echo" since the day in the lake. Dad had built a basketball court for us up by the house. It was here that Todd brought "Echo" up again.

"What I don't understand, Shawn," he said, "is why Mom and Dad haven't invited him to dinner. I mean, he speaks English and everything! We love it when people who speak English come to see us!" Todd had imagined "Echo" as an old hermit with a long gray beard living in the hills above our mission station with nothing better to do than copy the words we yelled out to him.

Todd's love of singing began as early as I can remember. Blessed with a booming voice, Todd had no need for a microphone. His career as a songwriter started at the tender age of three. He was always experimenting with new sounds and would compose long phrases he loved to roll off his tongue all throughout his boyhood. During our stay in the city of Kikwit, he asked me to write down the words of a song he had written. Having just reached his sixth birthday, he did not yet know how to read. This is the lyric I transcribed for him on paper that day:

> *God gave us our hands;*
> *God gave us our hands;*
> *And we love Him and adore Him,*
> *And we bow down before Him.*
> *God gave us our hands.*

The music, as usual, was already in his head.

Todd, Jack, and Dad returned to the Congo in 1997, when Congo was changing presidents. Local villages were spreading the rumor that Jim Smith would never be back to Nkara Ewa because of the country's unrest. Todd and Jack told Dad that the three of them needed to return to show the villages the Smiths had not left Congo. Left without transportation, the evangelism team, my brothers, and my dad walked ten miles one way to the village of Inimi to share the gospel. Todd and Jack both spoke to the people, and decisions were made for Christ. After the conclusion of the talk, the men walked ten miles back to Nkara in the dark. When the flashlight batteries failed, their Congolese brothers guided Dad, Todd, and Jack with the sound of their footsteps through the dark. The angels kept snakes and other wildlife from their path. The exhausted men safely arrived back at the mission station around 11 p.m. that night.

What I love most about my brother, Todd, is his compassionate heart. A time that vividly illustrates his heart to

Todd marries his bride, Angela Battiato, August 26, 2001.

me was when our dad was critically injured in Congo in 1989. Moments after receiving the early morning news of the accident, I rushed into his room, collapsing on his bedroom floor as I told him of the news. Todd bolted upright in bed and came over to me, holding me in his arms as I cried in fear. Todd kept his emotions in check, wanting to be a comfort to me, although I could see the panic in his own eyes.

The Lord has developed the gifts He has given Todd to minister to many. I am grateful for the blessing he has been to me. Toddy, I love you.

Chapter Eight

Precious Lord, Take My Hand

Mfumu Mfumu Simba Diboko

Every family tree has a branch that does not conform to the shape of the other branches. This is the branch that grows slightly crooked, has more bends in its length, and whose leaves may sprout in unexpected places. The other branches of the same tree may try to camouflage this branch occasionally out of embarrassment or lack of understanding. This sort of branch will rarely agree to just blend in. In the family tree of Laban and Marcella, their eldest son, Jack, represented this different sort of branch.

When Jack was two years old, Marcella caught sight of a green object protruding from her young son's nostril. Not knowing what it could be, she reached into Jack's nose and removed a leaf-sprouted corn kernel from where it had been lodged in his sinuses. Jack, unable to inform Marcella he had put it there because of his age, had been walking around with corn in his nose for weeks. This was only one of the many examples of unconventional behavior Jack would display in his childhood.

The Smiths returned to the United States for an eighteen-month furlough shortly after the end of World War II. In order to return to the Congo, the family had to endure several rounds of immunizations, some of which caused considerable

Precocious Jack with little brother Jim, 1945.

soreness at the injection site. Laban and Marcella were personal friends of the physician who administered the dreaded immunizations.

Jack had made up his mind he would not let anyone hurt him without a fight. Laban must have anticipated Jack's mindset. He realized that holding Jack on his lap might be the best solution for everyone involved. Syringes were made of glass in the 1940s. Jack saw the missile containing liquid pain coming straight for him and reacted with complete "Jack" logic. Before anyone knew what had happened, Jack shattered the glass syringe with the spoon he had hidden in his hand. Only after a stern reprimand and a second syringe did Jack get his necessary shot.

Congo was a boy's playground. Jack and his brother Jim thrived on the adventure that each new day promised. Unrestricted by traffic laws, Laban decided that Jack should learn to drive the pickup truck around the mission station to help him with different tasks. The thrill of being given such a grown-up privilege delighted nine-year-old Jack. The only activity as dear to Jack as driving was sucking his thumb, an activity my grandparents had vainly tried to get Jack to stop. Jack found he could maneuver the steering wheel with one hand and suck his favorite thumb on the opposite hand simultaneously. His father finally realized the only way to get Jack to give up sucking his thumb was to force him to choose between driving the truck or sucking his thumb. The truck won out.

Life was never boring with Jack's unending imagination to create fun. Jack's brother, Jim, was quieter and more compliant. He adored Jack and admired his brother's ability to bring excitement to their daily lives, but Jim was content to follow his big brother's lead into mischief rather than be its instigator. Jack was filled with the joy of life, with a heart that wanted to be good, even if his behavior did not always seem to match the desire of his heart.

The cruelty of life blindsided Jack like a head-on collision the day of his daddy's untimely death. Laban's fall turned the family's world upside down in an instant. Fun-loving, rambunctious Jack was trying to make sense of a tragedy that produced emotions his thirteen-year-old mind was incapable of processing. Jack was called upon to be the driver of the truck that carried his dying father to the hospital in Kikwit. The thrill of being behind the wheel was replaced with intense fear and dread. Driving would never have the same pleasure it once did after the sorrowful journey to Kikwit became part of Jack's memory.

After their father's death, Jack and Jim returned to the United States with their mother. Instead of the jungle of Congo, they now lived in the concrete jungle of the slums of Detroit. Jack was floundering. His inability to concentrate on his schoolwork led to failing grades. Nothing seemed to make sense to Jack except the ever-present companion of pain he had over Laban's death.

Marcella decided to put the boys in a Christian boarding school when she returned to Congo for eighteen months. Jack continued to perform poorly in school. It was not until a visit with his older brother, Herb, that Jack's life started to turn around. I do not know what was communicated during their time together, but the brothers' time together changed Jack's mindset. A newly found passion for the game of football gave him the focus he needed. Jack became a disciplined athlete and student.

Entering his junior year, Jack was a straight-A student and captain of his high school football team. Suffering had helped transform the rambunctious boy into a dedicated, godly young man. Time had dulled the ache caused by the void of his father. Jack could laugh wholeheartedly with his friends and experience the joy of living once again. By God's amazing grace, he had risen above the adversity and had found eternal treasures in the dark shadow of death.

One day that fall, Jack decided to go squirrel hunting with his brother, Jim. The two brothers decided to meet after circling a designated area of the woods. Jack went one way and Jim went in the opposite direction. Forty-five minutes later, Jim walked toward Jack, realizing Jack had

Learning to go on without Laban, 1954. Jack, Jim, Marcella.

never left the original location. Jim was about to vent his frustration to Jack when Jim sensed the hushed, meditative mood of his brother. Something profound and holy was silently taking place between Jack and the Lord. Jim stopped in his tracks, unable to interrupt the moment. No words were exchanged between the two of them as Jack and Jim returned to school.

The next evening, Jack and Jim and several of their friends decided to go camping in the Ozark Mountains some distance from their school campus. The young men tramped their way through the unbroken bracken of the woods to the small cave where they set up camp. Someone asked Jack to pray for the group, which he readily agreed to do.

"Lord, we pray for safety tonight, but how much more wonderful it would be to see Your face—and my dad's." Jack ended his prayer as the small group of boys scattered to prepare for their overnight stay under a sheetrock outcrop.

Some time later, Jack fell asleep under the ledge as Jim chopped wood for the campfire several feet away. Sudden fear gripped Jim as he heard the sheetrock creaking above Jack. Jim dropped his axe and ran to wake his brother. "Jack, Jack, wake up! It's not safe here; you have to get out!" Jim shouted. Jack assured his brother he would follow him out from under the ledge, but quickly went back to sleep. Jim heard the splitting of the rock and looked up just in time to see the ten-ton slab of rock crash down inches away as he turned his body to the left to escape. The rock completely covered the cave floor where Jack had been sleeping. An eerie silence entered Jim's ears.

The campsite was miles from the nearest help. Jim ran barefoot through the snow-covered broken branches and dead leaves, gashing his bare feet on stones and sticks in his desperate run for help for his brother.

Jack had always wanted to return to the land of his birth, where his father had given his life to bring the gospel to the Congolese people in Africa. Remembering the immense medical needs of the Congolese, Jack's desire was to become a missionary doctor. *Why, God, why?* Jim's mind was racing with the horror of the situation. Their father had been taken from them just five years earlier. Jim's shocked mind mercifully let him reject what he had just seen. He only focused on reaching help. Marcella met him on the stairs, with terror in her voice, demanding to know what had happened to her older son. "Mom, be calm . . ." Jim said.

Two days later, Jim and his mother sat numb with shock as they found themselves in the middle of Jack's memorial service. Jack's crushed body had been extricated from the rock that had taken his life and was now lying in a casket in front of the gathering of mourners. His death had been as unconventional as his life.

Jim knew he had a decision to make. In the days following the funeral, he offered God a challenge in an attempt to see if God was real. Jim vowed to give God one year to prove Himself. Jim committed to read the Scriptures daily for one year. "One year, Lord. I will give You one year. Show Yourself to me and I will follow You the rest of my life."

Jack's passion was to return to Congo to carry on the legacy of Laban and Marcella. In contrast to Jack, Jim had no desire to return to the country that had claimed his father's life.

Jeremiah 33:3 says, "Call to me and I will answer you and tell you great

John "Jack" Harold Smith (1939–1958).

and unsearchable things that you do not know." Jim found that the One who made this promise was faithful to fulfill the challenge Jim gave Him that day in 1958. The One whose hand Jim asked to take his has never been anything but faithful and has led him all the way.

Twenty years elapsed before Jim realized that the torch to reach souls in Congo, once so totally embraced by his parents, was being passed down to him. Jack's passion for carrying on the legacy was awakened in Jim's soul. The house fire we experienced in 1977 rekindled Jim's memories of his mother's peaceful reaction to the deaths of her husband and two sons and her faithfulness in returning to the country over the years with just $40 a month in financial support. Jim's last memory of Jack was his desire to return to the Congo. Jack could not return, and Jim, the only remaining child of Laban and Marcella, now felt the calling clearly. There were no other options. He must return to the land of his birth, the land and people of his father's eye, and the sacred ground of his childhood, where he was eyewitness to the Bayanzi awakening. Jim realized that the Lord's plan before the creation of the world was to have him put his hand to the spiritual plow and plant the seed of the Word of God in the soil of Africa enriched by his father's grave and to take up where his father had left off. Now Jim dared to pray for ten thousand souls in Congo for each of the family members God had taken from this life. This request has been granted by God in the thirty years since Jim returned to the work.

The sixteen-year-old boy that gave God the challenge was my father, the person blessed with the most childlike faith in his heavenly Father I have ever known. To be able to call him my dad is one of the greatest privileges I will ever call mine in this life.

Chapter Nine

Jesus Is Here

Yesu Azali Awa

How does a country that is not mine get into my blood and stay there no matter how much time has passed since I have been there? Even though the first four years of our stay in the Democratic Republic of Congo were marked with loneliness, homesickness, and culture shock, inevitably I think of our mission station, Nkara-Ewa, and its people every day. So much of my worldview has been shaped by the time I spent in the midst of a people of different skin color and language.

I have countless memories of my childhood, but there are some images that stay in my memory. They are like treasured items that bring their owner joy when they are brought out and looked at again. Somehow, time has a way of softening the rough edges of hard times, and transforming difficult times into memories of nostalgic joy.

Our parents purchased a 1957 seven-ton Mercedes Benz army truck we nicknamed the "Jolly Green Giant." This vehicle was our mode of transport over the roads of mud during the rainy season or the sand of the dry season. Some roads were little more than tire tracks in the savannah grasslands that we traversed back and forth to the nearest city of Kikwit or to one of the surrounding villages. Our favorite spot in the truck was a huge spare tire that was attached to the back of its cab. Nicol, Todd, and I would each try to scramble into the truck to get the coveted tire seat. Always, in case of a breakdown, five or more Congolese staff would hang on to the insides of the truck bed as we traveled at the "breakneck" speed of twelve miles an hour, bouncing down a road marked by potholes. Soon after starting on our journey, one of the Congolese would say to my brother, "Todd, yantika bankunga!" ("Todd, start the songs!") We would sing our way to our destination. Congolese music very often uses a form of song that designates one leader with the other singers repeating back what has just been sung. Todd most often was the designated leader with everyone echoing what he had just sung. Music was constantly in our lives. We learned very early in life the ability of a song to transcend barriers the spoken word might have.

Because we were the only missionary family on the station for much of our first three-and-a-half-year term, we were each other's playmates and companions out of necessity.

Out for a jaunt in the "Jolly Green Giant" army truck.

Every evening when Dad would turn the generator on for our evening ration of three hours of electricity, we would rush through the house to flip on every light switch. The house looked like a giant Christmas tree all lit up, which made us deliciously happy. Electricity meant we could use the 33-rpm record player my parents had brought especially for us. Some of our favorite albums were the Children's Hour *Tell Me a Story, Aunt B., Bing Crosby's Greatest Hits,* Bill and Gloria Gaither's children's albums, Ethel Barrett's spellbinding story albums, and an album of children's Christmas songs. We paid no attention to seasons. *Jolly Old Saint Nicholas,* along with the rest of the album's songs, could be heard on any given night from January to December. We would turn the volume up full-blast, bending over or falling on the floor from our gut-splitting laughter as we changed the normal speed of the record to either too fast or too slow. We would charge up and down the stairs and all through the house, singing along at the top of our lungs.

Every night our parents' bedroom became the center of family life for several hours until bedtime. If Dad and Mom were upstairs, none of us wanted to be downstairs in case an unwanted household guest in the form of a snake, bat, or rat came across our path. Our parents made us feel we were their most important priority, even above the work they had among the Congolese. They told us that constantly, but, more importantly, they lived that out in front of us. Because of their God-given wisdom in that perspective, I never felt their calling was my competition. We knew, because they honored their word to us so highly, they would pack up and leave Congo if one of their children could not cope with missionary life. God honored their faithfulness to us children and gave all of us kids grace to never ask to leave.

Those evenings as a family in their bedroom were days of training us in God's Word and talking through the loneliness we all felt in our isolation. Without fail, they would reassure us of their firm belief that God had called us to our new life. They allowed us to ask any question, always telling us that without our willingness to stay in Congo, they could not serve those to whom the Lord had called them to serve. This openness and affirmation from our parents created a motivation in us children to not approach them with much complaining about our lot. They made us feel that we were all in this together; we children had been called by God alongside our parents to serve the Congolese. We were a team.

Breakfast and lunch were always eaten together. Our breakfast usually consisted of homemade pancakes and fried canned ham. My mother learned to make her own version of granola. There is a saying that you know how many terms a missionary has been on the field by one's bowl of granola. The first-term missionary throws out the granola when it is realized the cereal contains bugs. The second-term missionary picks out the bugs, but wouldn't dream of throwing away the cereal. The third-term missionary looks for and misses the bugs if they aren't in the cereal. Powdered milk, something I never got used to, was the only choice of beverage besides water. We ate rice (bought in fifty-pound sacks) every day with some kind of creamed meat (canned tuna or ham usually) on top of it. Supper was usually a light meal, popcorn and hot chocolate, perhaps. There was not much variety in our diet, but God always supplied our daily bread.

The Word of God was always exalted in our home. Our parents talked so frequently about Christ that He was truly the invisible member of our family. From our earliest recollection, we knew He had died on the cross to bring salvation to the world. The most powerful and lasting lessons are caught, not taught. Our parents' lives have been a testimony to the Christ they have faithfully served all their lives. Dad and Mom were always careful to try to live out biblical truths they were trying to teach to us. They taught by example instead of by preaching at us. Nothing was beyond the need for prayer, whether it was for our safety through the day or for essentials such as food or fuel for the vehicles that could not be readily found. They continually modeled the importance of prayer. We children were privileged to see many answers to our parents' prayers. We were eye-witnesses to His power over and over again in our child-hoods, which gave us a wealth of experiences to draw from during crises of faith as individuals through our adolescence and adult years.

"By wisdom a house is built, and through understanding it is established; through knowledge its rooms are filled with rare and beautiful treasures." —PROVERBS 24:3–4

Our beautiful home at Nkara-Ewa built by Laban Smith in which his fatal fall occurred.

So many of my fondest memories revolve around the twenty-acre spring-fed lake in front of our home. The temperatures would soar over the 100-degree mark on the thermometer with the heat index and humidity in Congo where the equator crossed the map on the African continent. Our dad built a raft out of empty gas barrels and lumber that we would take out into the middle of the lake. Diving contests as well as games of tag and hide-and-seek were enjoyed daily in the water around the raft. All of us became strong swimmers who loved the water. Dad would join us in the late afternoons after working all day around the station or on his return from a trip off the mission station. Nicol, Todd, and I loved these times when all three of us would try to work together to dunk him under the water. One of us would get on his shoulders and the other two would grab one of his arms and try to pull him down under the water. We never could do it, but that never deterred us from trying the next time.

We had no television, very limited electricity, and the lake was our bathtub. We had none of the "necessities" for fun in the way of video games, computers, or DVDs that the majority of American children look to as a respite for boredom. We had to read and use our imaginations to come up with our own entertainment. Why do all of the memories I have recalled bring back such warm feelings of nostalgia and a longing for the simplicity of the life I knew as a child on the mission field? I am convinced it is because we knew Jesus was there with us. Those precious years as a family with very little outside distraction allowed us to be eyewitnesses to the truth that Jesus is very real and alive.

Looking back, He was present in every trip we took in the big Mercedes army truck. He protected us as the seven-ton truck rolled onto two logs, thinly disguised as bridges, which stretched across the waters of many streams. Although I remember our vehicle becoming stuck in the sandy or muddy trails that snaked the miles of savannah grassland we traveled, I never remember running out of fuel. Not once did we ever have an accident, and the only snakes we saw were ones that had already been killed. The Lord was the giver of the joy we felt as we sang our hearts out all over those roads. Those years of instruction and love from our parents allowed all of us to be able to cope with the separation we faced in attending a boarding school more than four hundred miles away from them in our junior high and high school years.

We need spiritually enlightened eyes to see the truth that He is always present, no matter how disappointing or joy-filled our circumstances may be. Jesus is the same yesterday, today, and forever—as present in our yesterdays as He is in our todays and tomorrows. Our times are in His hands.

> *Yesu azali awa! Yesu azali awa! Yesu azali awa na biso!*
> *Jesus is here! Jesus is here! Jesus is here with us!*
> —CONGOLESE HYMN (Author Unknown)

Chapter Ten

Poor, Wayfaring Stranger

Nzenza Mu Nzila

N icol, Todd, and I were ravenous after having just spent the morning playing in the lake at the bottom of the hill on which our home rested. The smell of freshly baked bread filled the house as we rushed upstairs to change out of our wet swimsuits. Nothing tasted better after a swim than that wonderful yeasty bread hot out of the oven. Our mouths watered in anticipation of biting into a large piece slathered with margarine and strawberry jelly. We often had a contest to see who could dress and be the first one down to the table. No prize was given to the winner, except the satisfaction that children receive from being able to shout, "I beat you!"

Our diet rarely changed. Our usual staple of white rice was on the table along with a dish of creamed ham to put on top of it. With the warm bread, we looked on this meal as a feast. Our hollow stomachs reminded us of the need to be fed. Because we rarely had fresh vegetables available to us, Mom had ordered canned peas and carrots from South Africa to supplement the need for the vitamins lacking in our diet. Nicol, having never been a picky eater, was nonplussed about eating those tasteless blobs that barely resembled real vegetables. Todd and I, however, could hardly choke them down. We would put those dreadful slices in our mouths and immediately reach for our water to wash their awful taste away. As soon as those were swallowed, the rest of the meal could be enjoyed.

"How can we get out of eating those yucky carrots, Todd?" Shawn and Todd, 1979.

I had just finished the unpleasant task of eating my carrots when we all heard a knock at the side door of the dining room. This was very unusual at mealtimes. My parents had asked the Congolese to respect our time together around the table for the noonday meal and not to knock on the door unless there was an emergency. When we first arrived, we felt as though we were on display, as our every move was monitored through their curious eyes. We had five large windows in the dining room around which both Congolese adults and children would crowd to watch us eat. Dad and Mom had allowed "the Smith show" to run for the first few weeks and then, respectfully but firmly, had asked our spectators to honor our need for privacy. Reluctantly, after many reminders, the Congolese acquiesced to our parents' wishes.

We children all groaned at the knock, wondering what need could possibly be so urgent that necessitated our meal being interrupted. Perhaps one of the most frustrating aspects of ministry in a Third-World country is that no matter how many needs are met, there are ten thousand that have not been met. It is like pouring a bucket of water on a raging forest fire. The needs never end nor lessen in their urgency. One need is as legitimate as the next, but resources are impossibly limited. It is an exhausting task to try to determine who needs what the most.

I could hear a man's desperate voice on the other side of the door. "Please, Madame [the title of respect the Congolese called my mother], please help me. I lost my wife to illness a while ago and my baby will not eat. I am afraid he is going to die. Please, please do something." As soon as we heard a baby was involved, all of us children got up from our seats and peeked around my mother to observe the situation. What we saw will be forever seared in my mind's eye.

The man's whole countenance was one of despair as he held out the pitiful bundle of skin and bones for us to gaze upon. Even we children could tell this infant's condition was far beyond any help my mother could offer him. Instead of the normal beautiful deep brown or black curliness, reddish-tinted hair topped this baby's head, a sure sign of malnutrition. The baby was so weak it could only stare out of huge, sunken eyes that seemed hollow and unearthly. He did not have the strength to even whimper. His abdomen was swollen in contrast to his sticklike limbs. Although he was around one year old, the age of our own baby brother, Jack, he looked as though he weighed no more than six to eight pounds. His father's desperate sobs shook his slender frame. Rarely have I seen such hopelessness since then.

As though heaven were crying with him, the sky opened up with large raindrops, thunder, and lightning. The church building was in the valley, and the man decided to wait out the rainstorm with his infant son in the shelter it would provide. My mother instructed him to come back to the house when the storm had passed, which the man agreed to do. With somber hearts, we stepped back into the dining room to get out of the rain and finish our meal. Although we had been famished when we sat down, we had all lost our appetite. None of us could take even a bite of the bread that had been so tempting before. We all feasted on our tears as we digested the cruel reality of what we had just seen. Nicol asked out loud what we all were trying to grapple with, "Mom, why did he wait so long to get help for his

The church building at Nkara-Ewa built by my grandmother, Marcella, after my grandfather, Laban, died.

baby?" My mother could not give a satisfactory answer and we did not demand one. We all knew Nicol's question was a rhetorical one.

The nearest hospital is a two-and-a-half-day walk for the villages surrounding Nkara-Ewa, representing more than two hundred thousand adults and their children. A walk of that length is daunting when one is healthy. When one is deathly ill, the option of either dying on the road or in the forest before reaching help makes the difficult journey incomprehensible for the Congolese. They choose to die at home in their villages surrounded by their family members. Preventative care is not part of their routine, as there are no clinics to meet even basic medical needs. Simple diseases, such as influenza, can wipe out entire villages of malnourished children as the illness ravages weak, starving bodies. A measles epidemic killed more than two hundred children in 1980 when I was twelve. I can still remember the mournful, haunting sound of the village drums beating out the death knell in the stillness of the African night as that village would announce the deaths of its children with each echo of the drum. The beating of the drums continued for more nights than I can remember. They stopped after my parents had an American nurse bring measles vaccine to our area to immunize a thousand children in an effort to stop the epidemic.

The rainstorm passed. We anxiously waited for the man to return with his baby as we prayed with our mom for wisdom to know how to help him. We felt helpless because the airstrip was not yet ready to fly the pair of them to the hospital in Vanga. I went out to sit on the side step of our house to wait for the man to come back with the baby. Looking down toward the valley at the church, I saw him walk out of the building with the baby lying in his arms. I watched as his dejected shoulders came closer as he approached the house. I called to my mom, and Nicol and Todd came out with her. The man was crying, but the tears seemed different. The look of desperation had gone out of his eyes, replaced by a look of shocked sorrow. The baby lay dead in his arms. Our tears joined his as we heard him say he was returning home to bury his baby.

Although the man probably gave his name that day, none of us remember it. The memory of the event has etched itself forever in my mind, but even the faces of that father and his infant son have faded into obscurity. I cannot conjure up their physical features anymore. I cannot, but Jesus looks on the face of that little soul that was lost to his father that day, which was raised to a life more glorious than I can imagine.

This life has irreconcilable injustices that I cannot fully rationalize in my mind. Why was our baby brother, Jack— the same age as that precious baby boy who died that day— born into a home where he would receive nourishment, medical care, and countless opportunities for a wonderful, comfortable life? We cannot choose our families or our socioeconomic standings. With some exceptions, most of us were born into comfortable circumstances in this country with amazing opportunities to continue bettering our lives. My mind will begin to reel if I try to make sense of the disparity between First-World and Third-World citizens.

I was privileged to grow up in an environment that forced me to have to grapple with these issues. The face of hunger lived right outside my front door. It was the frightening majority, not the minority that it is in my native land. I used to think I was rich in comparison to the Congolese and, materially, that is true. I have had to ask myself, however, what is true wealth? The Congolese know where their help comes from. They are some of the poorest people on this earth. They must look to their Creator for every need; and when He supplies those needs, He alone receives the glory. My material wealth has the capacity to make me spiritually poor. I can give myself undue credit for a comfortable life that I can falsely credit to a good education, sound financial decisions, or hard work. Not knowing where my help comes from makes me far poorer than that Congolese man will ever be. This is not heaven. Yet I demand so many times to have it all. Am I a poor wayfaring stranger to this world or have I become its friend, and in the process, not contemplated matters of eternal significance nearly enough? Do I anticipate heaven and God wiping away my tears one day as my Congolese brothers and sisters do? Or have my tears on earth been wept because of my spiritual poverty borne out of selfishly living for just me? Have most of my tears been over confusing my wants with my needs and my ungratefulness from ignoring how blessed I am?

The Congolese do not fear exchanging this life for heaven. They have real-life experiences that do not allow them the illusion that this world is anything more than a fleeting vapor. Indeed, it is the hope they cling to as they face unimaginable hardships. Those precious ones know that our real life is waiting to begin on the other side of eternity. This world of cruelty and hardship make them long for true riches, wealth that can never be taken away from them, earned by their faithfulness in believing they are just strangers passing through this world below. The best is yet to come. May God grant me the ability to not be deceived by the lie that this world should be what only heaven can offer, and may I live according to this truth that this world too often hides from me.

Chapter Eleven

I Bless Your Name
Mono Kumisa Zina Na Nge

It was Christmas 1981, and all of us kids were gathered in the living room around our artificial Christmas tree. The temperature, both indoors and outdoors, was probably in the high nineties; and the risk of sunburn instead of frostbite from the cold Decembers we experienced during our Michigan Christmases was now a reality. The adrenaline pumping through our veins at the thought of our new gifts was as great as at any other Christmas we could remember. We had decided to open the gifts in the evening because we could blast Christmas carols from our record player and have all the electric lights on in the house. We inhaled our Christmas dinner, which included an entire twelve-ounce bottle of Coca-Cola per family member—an unheard of treat reserved for extremely special occasions. Each of us kids took turns opening our gifts, as was the Smith family custom for unwrapping the shiny boxes under the tree.

Nicol and Todd opened their gifts with great delight. When my turn came to open one of my gifts, I realized I would have to try to hide my disappointment from all eyes that were on me. My first gift was a 1972 garage-sale special—a hideously ugly brown and white polka-dotted polyester dress. Every kid knows that brown is the worst color! I tried to feign excitement over this rare prize and smile through my sadness. I avoided my mother's eyes, knowing she would be able to see

Shawn, Nicol, and Todd in front of our palm-frond, sand-in-a-bucket Christmas tree, 1979.

right through my charade, and quickly said, with excitement I didn't feel, "Nic, it's your turn!" Again, Nicol and then Todd squealed with excitement over what their ripped-open packages revealed. I told myself I had gotten the worst of my presents out of the way and could now relax and enjoy what I would see in the packages under the Christmas paper. I carefully opened the wrapping to reveal a shirt with a picture of cavemen-like creatures chasing a wooly mammoth with spears. This could not be mine! No thirteen-year-old girl would have been caught dead in that shirt. I realized that the brown polyester dress was now the crown jewel of my gifts that year. I sat there utterly confused and disappointed at the injustice of my gifts in comparison to my siblings. Crazy thoughts started flooding my mind that my parents favored Nicol and Todd and that I was being punished for something. Were they playing some cruel joke on me? Not one gift that Christmas had come close to being a delight for me.

After all the gifts had been opened, I fled to my room upstairs to hide the sobs that were threatening to force their way from my throat. As I knew she would be, my mother was close behind. "Shawnee, honey, I gave some money to a lady in the States to buy gifts for all of you this year. The lady, in an effort to save money, told me she had done all of her shopping at garage sales, without asking me first. She was so proud she had saved us the money new gifts would have cost. Her heart was in the right place, but I wish she would have spent the money as I asked her to. I even gave her a list of what I knew all of you wanted. Nicol and Todd were happy with their gifts. The lady purchased the toys they wanted, but then decided to save money on the clothes I had asked her to get for you. Instead of using the clothing catalogue pictures I sent her as examples for what you wanted, she went to garage sales instead. I am so sorry, honey. I know how disappointed you are."

I sobbed into her shoulder as she cried along with me. There was nothing to be done and she and I both knew that. My mother had not been able to quickly run to the mall to pick up a few gifts to try to salvage my Christmas. She had been forced to watch me open one gift after another, knowing how devastated I would be with each one. In retrospect, her sadness was probably greater than mine, knowing she was unable to fix the situation, as I know her mama heart longed to do.

There are times in life that we expect a certain outcome, only to be devastated by reality. Nothing is more shattering emotionally than experiencing disappointment after trying to follow what we have believed is a solid plan for our lives. No daughter anticipates a mother dying three weeks after a brain tumor diagnosis. No eleven-year-old son is prepared to hear the words that his daddy, who was his hero, is now gone. No promising athlete with a full-ride scholarship foresees his or her dream of playing college sports ending with a devastating injury just weeks before training begins on campus. We can collapse emotionally under those circumstances that take our breath away as they turn our once safe and predictable world upside down. It is in those moments of intense inner turmoil and disappointment that we have a very difficult choice to make. Will we praise the One who has ordained every day of our lives before one came to be or will we not?

It is easy to praise my God when my road is level and stretches straight out in front of me, when His presence is so real I can almost touch Him, and when I know I am in the center of His will. The ability to rejoice in His goodness comes easily when my world makes sense to me.

However, when my world is rocked to its foundations by a situation that tests my belief in His goodness, feelings of hopelessness and anxiety can overwhelm me. When my mind is wreaking havoc on my emotions, when I don't want to obey, when troubles are all around me, when I can't see His face, when I don't know I am in the center of His will even though I am so desperately seeking that, I can feel as powerless to change my situation as a prisoner in chains is to unlock her shackles.

Psalm 50:23 has become such a powerful tool in combating the prison the enemy of my soul would like to keep me in. It says, "He who sacrifices thank offerings honors me, and he prepares the way so that I may show him the salvation of God."

Christmas 1981 was as profound a disappointment to me as my thirteen-year-old mind could imagine at that point in my life. I did not know how to praise Him then for that circumstance. Only recently have I taken God at His Word, as I have chosen to apply the promise of Psalm 50:23 to those situations that make praising Him difficult. I have

Leaving Nkara-Ewa for furlough in the United States, May 1982. Left to right: Nancy, Jim, Shawn, Jack, Todd, Nicol.

been astounded at what has happened. I used to think my world would only be right again if the difficulty I was facing turned in my favor. The paradox I have found is that the adverse circumstances have not always changed, but that my sacrifice of praise has freed me from their power to shackle me in the chains of despair. I need to praise the Lord, not for His sake, but to remind me that He is greater than any disappointment, worry, or fear I may have. His presence is what I am looking for the most. He promises He inhabits the praises of my lips. I have found that promise to be true when I bless His name and wait to see His salvation.

Chapter Twelve

Be Thou My Vision
Vanda Lutala Na Mono

"Be Thou my vision, O Lord of my heart. Naught be all else to me save that Thou art . . ." —IRISH HYMN

M y grandmother, Marcella, had a beautiful voice and loved to sing the hymns. As a young girl, I remember her singing the refrain of one particular hymn called "Jesus Doeth All Things Well." I could

Marcella Smith at Nkara-Ewa, 1969.

not understand then, listening to her soprano voice, what a sacrifice of praise that song must have been for her to sing.

Forced to leave her life of ministry in the Congo in 1953, in which she and her husband Laban had witnessed the glorious life-changing power of Christ in the Congolese, the ensuing years of my grandmother's life were marked with intense suffering. With only a fourth-grade education and no real ability to provide materially for her two sons, Jack and Jim, she and the boys lived with a single woman in a poor part of Detroit for the first two years following Laban's death. Marcella's heart continued to be with those she and her husband had served. In 1955, she returned alone to the Congo for eighteen months to oversee the work they had started among the Congolese. She was forced to leave her sons at a Christian dormitory in Wheaton, Illinois.

Smith Family at Iwungu, 1947. Left to right: *Laban, Marcella, Jack, Jim.*

When she returned to the States in 1956, she became a dorm mother in exchange for tuition for Jack and Jim at the Bible Institute of the Ozarks. It was during her tenure there she experienced burying a child for the second time. Her eighteen-year-old son, Jack, was killed on a camping trip in 1958. She continued alone to return to the Congo throughout the 1960s to carry out the vision she and her late husband had been given. Many of those years, she survived on the forty-dollar per month support she received from her niece in the United States. Marcella continued her work in Africa until stomach cancer forced her to return to the States in 1971.

After much of her stomach was surgically removed, she returned to the home of the single woman in Detroit with whom she and her sons had lived right after the death of my grandfather. With so little formal education and now in her late sixties, she was forced to go on government aid to survive.

In 1976, my grandmother moved into a mobile home on the property our parents had bought in western Michigan. She received burns on her hands as she tried to put out the fire that destroyed her trailer in February of 1978. My parents' home had also been lost to a fire the previous November through which my parents received the call to go back to the Congo. Overjoyed that her one surviving child was now going to carry on the work started by his father and mother, my grandmother left this country in October of 1978 to go back to the Congo to make preparations for our family's new life there.

Within the first week of our family's arrival to the Congo in December 1978, my father received the shocking news that she had been buried for three weeks. She had died alone in a bedroom downstairs in the home where her husband had fallen during its construction. The Congolese had taken her body and buried her yards away from my grandfather's grave in a small cemetery in the city of Kikwit. A simple cross made out of sticks of wood marked the fresh mound of dirt.

It seemed a tragic way for a woman so faithful to her calling to leave this world, but that judgment was made without spiritual understanding. Her life was one of sacrifice, hardship, and obscurity. She experienced very few of earth's comforts. She died with no family around her in an environment very taxing to her physically.

Although my grandmother died alone on a remote African bush mission station, she did not die distraught. This woman who so dearly loved the Scriptures left her earthly tent believing in the promise given to her in Job 19:25–27:

> *"I know that my Redeemer lives, and that in the end he will stand upon the earth. And after my skin has been destroyed, yet in my flesh I will see God; I myself will see him with my own eyes—I, and not another. How my heart yearns within me!"*

The very suffering Marcella endured allowed her to receive spiritual eyes. Knowing this world was not her home, she made a deliberate decision of her will to continue serving her King. Although she lost her life partner and had experienced the grief of having to bury two children, she did not grieve as those with no hope. She knew she only had one life to live for her Savior and chose, through all of the suffering, to faithfully serve her Lord. Jesus had told her in John 16:33: "I have told you these things, so that in me you may have peace. In this world you will have trouble. But take heart! I have overcome the world." Marcella Smith's vision was not on her earthly circumstances, but on the One who gave her the privilege of sharing in His sufferings.

Enter through the narrow gate. For wide is the gate and broad is the road that leads to destruction, and many enter through it. But small is the gate and narrow the road that leads to life, and only a few find it. —MATTHEW 4:13–14

Jesus beckons each one of us to enter the narrow gate that leads to the life few find. My grandmother entered the gate that few choose. The sacrifice this way demands is considered too high a price to pay by many. Her life was a sacrifice of sweet savor on the altar to the One who was her vision.

Visiting Grandma Smith's grave at Kikwit Cemetery, 1979. Left to right: *Nicol, Shawn, Todd, Nancy* (holding Jack).

Marcella Smith left nothing of earthly value to her off-spring. Upon her death, our family did not inherit a large bank account, expensive furniture, or a recognizable family name. Yet, as I view the life of faith she lived before her Savior, I stand in awe of the legacy she has left to me. Her life calls to me to choose carefully the path I take in Jeremiah 6:16: "This is what the LORD says: 'Stand at the crossroads and look; ask for the ancient paths, ask where the good way is, and walk in it, and you will find rest for your souls . . .'"

Although I have nothing tangible to remember her by, the life she lived in obedience is of inestimable worth. She gave everything to the One to whom she owed so much. As I stand at my own crossroads in my relationship to the Lord, I have only to look at the lives of my grandparents as I evaluate the cost of following in their footsteps. The ancient good path is lined with suffering. I thank God for the courage He gave my grandmother to continue serving Him with no bitterness after her earthly life seemed to fall apart. Marcella Smith's eyes were not on her suffering, but on Jesus, the Author and Perfecter of her faith. The joy of heaven was ever before her as she made Christ her vision. Was following her God worth the cost? I know her answer to me would be found in her joyful praise:

> *High King of heaven, my victory won,*
> *May I reach heaven's joy, O bright heaven's Sun!*
> *Heart of my own heart, whatever befall,*
> *Still be my Vision, O ruler of all.*
> —IRISH HYMN, Translated by Mary Elizabeth
> Byrne (1880–1931)

Chapter Thirteen

When I Survey the Wondrous Cross

Bu Mono Tala Kulunʃi Kitoko

"When I survey the wondrous cross on which the Prince of glory died . . ."   —ISAAC WATTS

The telephone rang only once, causing both my mother and me to spring up out of bed from a sound sleep. I glanced at the clock, which read 1:45 a.m. What good news comes at that hour of the morning? An icy dagger of fear pierced my heart as I heard my mother's voice confirm this was bad news. "Kathy, is he alive?" her voiced was thick with fear and imminent tears. Our worst fears had been realized: My father had been involved in a life-threatening automobile accident. Dad was eight thousand miles away in Congo with some of his cousins, who were there to put the roof on the newly constructed Bible school building at Nkara-Ewa. My mother was scheduled to join him in a matter of days with a team of people going to Nkara-Ewa from the United States. My sister, Nicol, was in France studying the French language for college credit. My brothers, Todd and Jack, were accompanying my mother to Congo for the summer. I was going to be the only family member to be left at home in the States, where I was employed for the summer.

Jim marries Nancy McKown, August 15, 1964. Left to right: Grandpa McKown, Grandma McKown, Nancy, Jim, Aunt Gerry and Uncle Paul with Mark and Terri.

Now, in a matter of seconds, our plans had changed. Great stress and tragedy have a way of burning emotions and fears that stay etched forever in one's memory. We learned in that phone call that our family had forever been changed. We were about to embark on a new sense of normal, which included a father with a closed head injury lying in a filthy, incompetent African hospital far away. Helplessness threatened to smother me that night like a pillow held over my face.

My mother and brothers flew out on the next available flight to Congo after an emergency meeting with my parents' friends and board of directors at four o'clock in the morning. The next few days were a blur. My name was transferred onto another team member's ticket, which allowed me to go in place of her. I had to fly to New York and stay with a family on Long Island to obtain a tourist visa. I do not remember very much about that time, as my thoughts were constantly with my father. Would he look any different? Would he survive? Were people taking care of him in our family's absence? I boarded the plane and spent the longest eighteen hours of my life trying to get to him. I dared not let my mind wander to the horrible possibility of not getting to the Congo before he died. Through many tears, I begged the Lord to let me see him at least one more time alive.

As I sat in the cramped airline seat, I struggled with the seeming injustice of the frightening circumstances in which I suddenly found myself. My father had always been my hero. Never once had he shaken a fist at God over being the sole survivor of his immediate family. My grandfather, Laban, grandmother, Marcella, and two uncles, Jack and Gareth, had all gone on to be with the Lord. Only my grandmother, Marcella, had lived into her seventies. The other three members of his family had died untimely deaths. In spite of great personal suffering, my dad had lived his life in gratitude toward God rather than in bitterness. The thought that God may be asking me to relinquish my forty-seven-year-old father to death was unthinkable. I told God I would do anything for Him, but that I did not know if I could bear losing my father. "Please, Lord, don't ask me to do this," I whispered through the sobs I was trying to stifle in the small airline pillow.

It was not until I had arrived in the Congo, now ten days after the accident, that I heard the full details of the accident. The year of 1989 had not yet seen the arrival of international cell phones or e-mail that could have kept us up-to-date with the latest information on Dad's condition. I breathed a sigh of relief when my mother told me he was still living.

The day after my arrival, my mother told me the details of the accident. She asked my brothers and me if we wanted to go see the vehicle involved in the crash. I adamantly refused. With my father's condition so precarious, I did not want to face the twisted metal and allow that image to become part of my memory. The roof of the Isuzu Trooper that my father and a fellow missionary had been driving in looked like the lid of a tin can that had been peeled back. Returning to the capital city of Kinshasa after sending his cousins on ahead to our mission station of Nkara-Ewa, he and the other gentleman had slammed into a trailer-tractor truck bed that had pulled unexpectedly across the two lanes on their side of the divided road. The driver of the other truck was drunk. There was no shoulder for Dad and Tim Downs to try to pull onto to avoid this obstacle in their path. The Trooper went directly underneath the truck bed.

Convinced that both my father and the other man were dead, some Congolese onlookers stripped my father of most of his clothing, stealing his camera, cash, and other personal belongings while he lay unconscious. The accident had occurred right outside the gate of the national army barracks. A French doctor who happened on the scene asked if anyone knew how to operate the only crane in the city, located at the adjoining airport. Not only did someone know how to operate it, but in this country of rationed gasoline, the crane actually could be started. It took four hours for the crane to lift the truck bed off the Trooper in order to safely extricate my father and Tim. After finally reaching the men in the midst of the twisted steel and finding them miraculously alive, the doctor stabilized my father and called in to the Congo-American clinic with the news that two American missionaries had been seriously injured.

The missionary community immediately responded, lining up to donate blood, which was not necessary in the

The demolished Isuzu Trooper that almost claimed my father's life, 1989.

end. After being informed of the accident, Kathy Kirkpatrick went to a mutual friend's home to place the jarring early morning phone call to my mother.

My father was transferred to Ngaliema Hospital to be under the care of both Belgian and Congolese doctors. The hospital was a pit of filth and disease. The dictator of the country, Mobutu Sese Seko, refused to give money to adequately staff or provide even the basic services that First-World countries provide to patients. He preferred to line his own pockets with foreign-aid money that poured into Congo. We believe that my father contracted hepatitis B at Ngaliema through contaminated syringes that had been used repeatedly by the hospital's staff on its patients.

I remember the smells of that dreadful hospital ward as I saw the shocking form of my father lying in one of the beds. The pungent odors almost overwhelmed my senses as I tentatively laid a hand on my father's arm, not knowing if I would hurt him. His face was covered in lacerations and the right side of his face was black and blue. I had always seen my father as a pillar of strength. Now he was showing the frightening truth of his fallibility as he wept and asked the same questions of us repeatedly. He had no idea where he was and kept begging us to take him out of that hospital. The panic in his voice shook my world to its very foundation. I was in the middle of a nightmare of role reversal, having to assure my father that we were there with him and were not going to leave him. He knew all of us, but I could tell something traumatic had happened to his brain.

Three weeks later, after brain scans and many consultations with a wonderful Congolese neurosurgeon, Dad was ready to be medivaced home to the United States. Dr. Sylvia Hartog refused to accept any money toward the cost of her flight to accompany my parents back to the United States. Her presence was required throughout the entire journey. Dr. Hartog flew from Congo to Detroit and admitted my father to William Beaumont Hospital. After my father's hospital admission, she flew back to Congo. We were unable to adequately thank her for the tremendous blessing she had been to my parents. Todd, Jack, and I were left behind in Congo to see my father's cousins off on their flight back to the United States. The boys and I left the country several days later.

Returning to the United States was the beginning of a long, painful, and sometimes humiliating rehabilitation for my father. Nerve damage caused a sharp and constant tingling sensation in his left leg, making it difficult for him to stand from a sitting position. As is typical with a closed-head injury, there was frustration on his part at having to deal with short-term memory loss that caused him to ask the same questions many times. My mother's marriage vows were put to the test as the "for better" part of her life with my dad turned, for a season, to "the worst" part of it. She faithfully stood by his side through all of it.

American culture worships at the shrine of comfort and leisure. I realize how much I have bought into the lie that following Christ should be a continual joyride, free from suffering. In fact, as I now analyze the bargaining I did with God during the airplane ride to the Congo to see my injured father, my sense of injustice over the situation came from the fact that my idea of fairness was not based on the picture of following Christ that Scripture says is the truth found in Matthew 16:24–25:

> *Then Jesus said to his disciples, "If anyone would come after me, he must deny himself and take up his cross and follow me. For whoever wants to save his life will lose it, but whoever loses his life for me will find it."*

The truth I must realize is that Jesus requires those who love Him to lead a life which includes a cross. There was no glory in those pieces of wood to which the body of my Savior was nailed. The agony of the cross, however, provided the way for this sinner to be called a child of God. The glory of the cross is found not in its physical attributes, but in what it accomplished, allowing me to cross from death to life as I believe in the power of the cross to save me from God's wrath. Why does my foolish heart not see the cross Jesus has asked me to take up as a privilege, not a curse? The cross is not a thing to avoid. The suffering of the cross Jesus has asked me to take up is the means by which I become more like Him!

There is no denying my father's accident was a cataclysmic event in our lives. In fact, our family refers to our lives lived together as "pre-accident" and "post-accident." My father's life was forever altered. Though his injured brain has been miraculously healed, and it is not physically apparent that he was involved in a nearly fatal collision, the road to recovery was tedious and required consistent surrender to God's will. He determinedly exchanged the constant temptations of depression, bitterness, and anxiety for the mind of Christ throughout his recovery. Therefore, by the grace of God, his self-pity was short-lived by daily recounting the promises of God instead of listening to the lies of Satan. He continues to be a testimony to the fact that, with God, all things are possible. My father has never been more focused on the work God has called him and my mother to do. There is something urgent in the way he lives his life and his zeal for his Savior. The cross Christ required him to take up has demanded much from him personally. Christ has been worthy of the cost.

> *Were the whole realm of nature mine,*
> *that were a present far too small;*
> *Love so amazing, so divine,*
> *Demands my soul, my life, my all.*
> —ISAAC WATTS (1674–1748)

Chapter Fourteen

Sweet, Sweet Song of Salvation

Ntomo Ntomo Nkunga Mpulusu

The LORD is my strength and my song; he has become my salvation. Shouts of joy and victory resound in the tents of the righteous: "The LORD's right hand has done mighty things!"
—PSALM 118:14–15

A song starts with one note, needing one singer to announce its beginning and existence. The first singers of the song of salvation to the Bayanzi people of the former Belgian Congo were Dr. Laban and Marcella Smith in 1947. For the next five years, the singers of the song would swell to more than ten thousand people as they found Jesus Christ to be the source of their salvation. The momentum and volume of the song seemed to be at a crescendo when, in 1953, Dr. Smith suddenly lost his earthly life. Would the song, once so vibrant, be still forever? From an earthly perspective, the sweet song had been silenced as Marcella had to pack up her two boys and leave the country's soil in which her husband was now buried.

In 1978, our family arrived in the Democratic Republic of Congo to find that our grandmother Marcella, who had returned to the country ahead of us, had been buried just three weeks before. My parents had been called to pick up the work Laban and Marcella Smith had started almost twenty-five years before.

The dictator of the country, Mobutu Sese Seko, forbade the building of decent roads for fear of being invaded by enemy armies. Surrounding our station were dirt paths, not worthy of being called roads, which had to be traversed in difficult conditions. No service stations or roadside assistance was available along the way to the villages surrounding our mission station.

Evangelism is the heart of Laban Ministries. The desire to reach the Bandundu province with its own men and women trained in the Scriptures was the reason for the founding of Laban Bible Institute. The over five hundred

Dr. Laban Smith Family Prayer Card Photo, 1946. Left to right: *Laban* (holding Jim), *Marcella* (holding Baby Gareth), *and Jack.*

graduates of the school's two campuses attended with the knowledge that the song of salvation would have to be carried by foot to those with whom it was being shared. Many of the graduates would walk tens if not hundreds of miles to attend class, knowing full well there would be no vehicle to help them in their future ministries. In 1981, three years after their arrival in the Congo, my parents started praying for God to give them a radio station whose airwaves would spread the gospel of Jesus Christ to areas inaccessible by foot or vehicle.

Nkara-Ewa was in a lush valley surrounded by horseshoe shaped hills. After being granted permission by the governor of the province of Bandundu, East Hill was chosen to be the spot for the future radio station that my parents, in faith, believed the Lord would give them. Faith was all they had at that time because of the tremendous obstacles that stood between the dream of the station and its reality. There were no funds, only the promise that God exalts His Word above all else along with the faith that He would remove all the impediments.

In 1997, sixteen years after the vision for the radio station was given, Jack and Nita Westerbeek of Grosse Ile, Michigan, stood on the top of East Hill and covenanted with the Lord to give the funds necessary for the radio station and tower to be built. Jack had contracted non-Hodgkin's lymphoma two years before and prayed that he would live to be able to see the tower standing on the hill allowing the gospel of Jesus Christ to be proclaimed to the Congolese. The Lord's perfect plan for Jack Westerbeek was to come home to Himself in November of 2003, eight months before the tower's completion.

A three-hundred-foot tower was purchased from Pyrod in 2001 and in the next two years, the Lord brought together his people in the United States to finance the shipping of two forty-foot containers. Contents of the container included the radio tower, two army trucks, a backhoe, and various pieces of equipment needed to erect the tower more than eight thousand miles away from its origination point in Indiana. In 2003, the containers were shipped to Baltimore and put on a ship that would take them across the Atlantic Ocean to the Congo port of Matadi.

Once in Matadi, a trucking service brought the containers to the capital city of Kinshasa. The two army trucks had to be unpacked and reassembled from the containers that held them. A company in Kinshasa had reassured my dad the company's crane was adequate in lifting the containers from the trucks onto the barge from Matadi. While they were able to lift the container holding the radio tower, which came within eight inches of falling into the Congo River, the other container, which had been so carefully packed, had to be completely unpacked, lifted off the truck, and repacked. The tower container was finally loaded onto another barge in Kinshasa bound for Pindi, a town about twenty miles away from our mission station of Nkara-Ewa.

No trucking company exists in Pindi, so the unpacked, reassembled army trucks, had to travel from Kinshasa over four hundred miles to unload the contents of the second container at Nkara before they could retrieve the tower container. However, because of no maintenance on the only paved stretch of road built in the 1970s between Kinshasa and Nkara-Ewa, that need translated into a four-day trip of dodging potholes in a road lined with bandits. God's people were praying.

Another thing lacking in the town of Pindi was a port! Two weeks after arriving at Nkara, the unloaded army vehicles were sent to Pindi. Six-inch thick boards, one end resting on the barge and one end on the truck bed, were used to load the containers from the barge onto the vehicles. Surely

Jim Smith Family Prayer Card Photo, 1987. Left to right (standing): *Shawn, Todd, Nicol.* Left to right (sitting): *Jack, Jim, Nancy.*

the angels were orchestrating every move, as one slip could have sent the tower into the muddy waters of the Kwilu River.

Six miles away from the station, one of the trucks hit a sandbank and flipped on its side. Miraculously, the steel of the tower was unscathed, and the trucks arrived at the site on East Hill that had been designated for the radio station.

In July 2004, twenty-four years after the vision was given to make it possible for the song of salvation to be heard on the airwaves, the Radio Nkembo became a reality. Today, Radio Nkembo (Radio Glory) is heard as far as the capital of Kinshasa, the country of Angola, and Brazzaville, a potential audience of five million people. A vehicle cannot go where a radio can. Villagers who have not yet had an evangelism campaign are hearing the gospel as they go about their day. Only eternity will tell the impact of the song of salvation that some are hearing for the first time.

The best songs have a sampling of both dissonant and harmonious chords, which allows the listener to be awed by the full range of their majestic sound and power. The first note of the song of salvation was sung to the Bayanzi people in 1947 by Laban and Marcella Smith, who had found the song to be so sweet they could not keep it to themselves. The song has had its dissonant chords, some of which stayed unresolved for many years. It required the ultimate sacrifice from both of them—their very lives. My grandfather Laban's untimely death in 1953 seemed to hush the song for twenty-six years. Our grandmother, Marcella, was also required by God to lay down her life for His beloved ones in Congo. Yet, almost thirty years after our parents' own arrival to the Congo and their continuation of the ministry, we can see the song of salvation was not silenced or stopped. The One who had started the good work in Laban and Marcella is still faithfully completing it to this very day.

We must listen to a song in its entirety before we can judge whether it is poorly or masterfully crafted. We cannot take one line or bar of music and make an evaluation of the entire song on just that one section. We must know the beginning from the end. We do know the beginning from the end of the song of salvation.

> *Then I heard every creature in heaven and on earth and under the earth and on the sea, and all that is in them, singing: "To him who sits on the throne and to the Lamb be praise and honor and glory and power, for ever and ever!"* —REVELATION 5:13

What does your life's song sound like right now? Perhaps the song of your life with Jesus is harmonious, like a beautiful symphony with all of its various parts singing together wonderfully well. However, there may be some of us who have lately hit a dissonant chord and have taken our recent trial out of the context of the whole song of our lives. We have become discouraged and have maybe evaluated our whole life's song as being a failure instead of the masterpiece God has the ability to make it. At those times, we must remember this:

> *In him we were also chosen, having been predestined according to the plan of him who works out everything in conformity with the purpose of his will, in order that we, who were the first to hope in Christ, might be for the praise of his glory.*
> —EPHESIANS 1:11–12

Our great God has the power to use both the beautiful and dissonant chords of our lives and bring them into conformity with His perfect plan. All the notes are needed to sing the sweet, sweet song of salvation.

Chapter Fifteen

Amazing Grace
Lemvo Ya Yituka

" 'Twas grace that taught my heart to fear and grace, my fears relieved . . . ." —JOHN NEWTON (1725–1807)

Our childhoods were full of moments of grace. I sometimes let my mind run through halls of memories built around my years growing up in the Congo. Although life certainly had its challenges because we lacked many of those things deemed absolutely essential, like running water and twenty-four-hour electricity, there are moments frozen in time that bring pure joy to me when I remember them.

I had been an extremely finicky eater before we moved to Congo. The foods on my plate could not touch at all or I would not eat any of them. It is amazing how hunger motivates one to eat those things that were thought of before as detestable. We had been in the Congo for three months and had just moved to Kikwit, the city nearest our mission station of Nkara-Ewa. We had stopped in Kikwit for a short time before we went on to the mission station. The Congolese love everything cooked well done or burned to a crisp. My mother tried, unsuccessfully, to explain to Solomon, the Congolese man who prepared our meals, that we liked our toast golden brown. Every morning, without fail, he would burn the toast to a blackened crisp before he slapped lard on it. The first few days, I refused to eat it. On the fifth day, even black toast started to appeal to my taste buds. Our grandmother, Marcella, had sent a package from the United States before her departure to Congo. Four months after her death and three months after our arrival, the package came. I do not remember anything else in the package except for the envelope of Lawry's brown gravy mix she had packed. Todd, Nicol, and I literally danced around the table that day knowing we would have packaged brown gravy on our plain white rice. We could not believe how rich we were to be able to indulge in such a feast.

It was in Kikwit that we met Gary Kapinga, who is now the national director of Laban Ministries in Congo. He was a mere boy, barely out of his adolescent years, at our first introduction. Gary helped Solomon prepare the meals in the kitchen of the guesthouse in Kikwit. Unheard of luxuries, such as Golden Delicious apples and fruit cocktail, could be ordered in food shipments from South Africa. My mother and I tore open the wonderful boxes containing these delights on the day of the arrival of our first food shipment. I could not keep myself from squealing with utter joy over the can of fruit cocktail that was on the top layer of one of the food shipment boxes. I ran to Nicol and Todd to share my excitement over the fact that Mom had said we could eat the whole can with our lunch of white rice and canned corned beef. Being just ten years old at the time, I mistakenly assumed Gary would know how to prepare this treat. To him, everything in a can was supposed to be cooked in a pan on the stove. He proceeded to open the can and cook the fruit cocktail. Our mouths were watering in the dining room as he proudly brought the pan to the table. We all dissolved in a flood of tears over hot fruit cocktail, leaving poor Gary shaking his head. His distress to our reaction was as great as our disappointment.

Our beloved Gary Kapinga, present-day International Director of Laban Ministries, with his wife, Jean, and children.

Two years later, when I left to attend a boarding school for missionary children in northwestern Congo, my parents let Nicol have a white-nosed monkey to help with the loneliness she experienced during the year she and I were apart. Our dad once had a monkey of the same species when he was a boy in Congo. Nicol decided to name her monkey after the one my father had during his childhood. T.D. adored my sister, but *only* her. She would crochet little yarn diapers for him (yes, they were as useful in their purpose, as one may imagine), let him sleep in her room with her, and carry him in her arms everywhere she went on the mission station. If any other family member dared to touch him, we were rewarded with a bite to the hand. Nicol would chide T.D., but I always thought she secretly relished his total devotion to her.

Before our arrival at the mission station of Nkara-Ewa, our home had been occupied by seven Congolese families.

Besides their children, these families had let their live-stock—goats, chickens, and sheep—wander through the home at will. No section of the house, either upstairs or downstairs, was off limits to these critters. After we had moved in, my mother laid down the law, in no uncertain terms, that these feathered and four-legged creatures had received their eviction notice. One black hen, however, re-fused to acknowledge my mother was now the mistress of the house. On a daily basis, the hen tried to nest in my bedroom located on the second floor. Mom would shoo the hen through the unscreened windows in my bedroom with her broom and quickly pull the wooden shutter closed after it, only having to repeat the very same process the follow-ing day.

My room had the only entrance to the attic, where we kept items in storage. A wooden ladder was built into the wall across from my bed that allowed access into the rat-infested quarters above. I would listen to the rodents having races across my plywood ceiling panels, always wondering what would happen if one of them fell down the open space in the ceiling where the ladder was. Thankfully, I never was aware if this occurrence became a reality.

We had to make up our own fun. My sister and I had a stint of making bread to sell to the Congolese. Looking back, I am amazed our mom let us make these yeast concoc-tions, many of them total failures, with our pantry's limited resources of the dry ingredients they required. We sold more than one brick loaf to people on the mission station, thinking we were quite the accomplished culinary artists.

I adored the piano and played every chance I could in any missionary home that had one. I was thrilled when my parents acquired a piano for our home, which they had purchased from an American family who had left Congo for good. The humidity caused the middle-C key to stick as though it were being played. A small, lit kerosene lantern was placed in the bottom section of the instrument to help alleviate this problem. The timing of the song was always a little off, as I had to pick up the middle-C key and then play it during the talent shows and recitals we would have for each other in our living room. It was at this piano that our family would sing the old hymns together that came to mean so much to us.

"Tag, anyone?" The raft at Lake Ewa on which we spent countless hours playing.

My grandfather had built two homes on the mission station. In 1981, the Rouster family joined us at Nkara, living in the "white" house, the first house my grandfather had built on the station. A circular driveway separated the two homes. One of my favorite memories was dressing up in homemade costumes, using whatever we could find, and going to the eight doors between the two houses to trick-or-treat. My mom and Aunt Lorella Rouster handed out goodies at each of the doors as we circled both of the homes' exteriors.

The Congolese diet consisted of a paste-like substance made from cassava root that they dipped into the cassava plant's leaves as the staple for every meal they ate. I never liked the taste of either one. Warm luku, in my opinion, was horrid tasting enough; when it was cold, it was truly awful. My mom, Nicol, and I secretly decided to play a trick on the Rouster kids. Every Christmas, my mother would make Russian teacake cookies, which were butter cookies rolled in powdered sugar. We decided the last door visited at our home would be the trick door. We had taken cold luku and rolled it in flour. The deceptive appearance made us giggle with delight as we anticipated the response a bite of one of these would get from the eater. Tears of laughter rolled down our cheeks as the response was better than we had anticipated from the unfortunate one who bit into our awful "cookie."

During our second term as missionaries, our family welcomed a chimpanzee named Chico into our family. Chico never realized he was not a human being. We kept a case of Coca-Cola, containing twenty-four bottles, up in the attic. With soft drinks or sugary treats of any kind being so difficult to come by, this case was completely off-limits to us, except for special occasions. I remember one day my parents opening up one bottle and all six of us sharing it. All of us kids were in awe of the fact we each got to drink several sips of Coca-Cola for no special reason.

Chico loved Coca-Cola as much as we did. He would sneak into the house and find his way into my bedroom, which contained the entrance to the attic. Chico always managed to find the soda case no matter where we hid it. Not needing a can opener, he would use his teeth to pop off the top of the bottle. I had just gone into my room one day when I heard a strange sound coming from the attic. Climbing up the ladder to the attic, my eyes widened at what I saw. There sat Chico, completely oblivious to my presence, starting on the second half of the Coca-Cola case with the first twelve bottles, now empty, strewn all around him. The strange sound I had heard was the expulsion of the carbonation from his throat!

Dad holding the cola-loving chimpanzee, Chico.

The summer of my junior year of high school, Todd, Nicol, and I invited twelve missionary kids from our school in Kinshasa to visit us at Nkara-Ewa for a week. We had so much fun swimming in the lake and diving off the raft, sitting around a bonfire one night, and doing the "I Wish I Were a Missionary Kid" skit for the adults. The highlight of the week together, however, was the zip line that Dad set up for us. He strung the wire, attached on either end to the bumper of a vehicle, the entire length across the lake and fastened a handle to it so we could run down the hill to pick up speed before we dropped into the lake. He had placed a knot in the middle of the wire above the deeper water. All of us spent hours taking turns running down the hill, holding onto the wire, and competing to see who could hold on to the handle the longest before dropping into the water. I was so proud my father saw this work on his part as ministry to our friends and to us.

My response to all of these wonderful experiences in my childhood is one of amazement. John 1:16 says, "From the fullness of his grace we have all received one blessing after another."

Did I always recognize God's amazing grace as I was experiencing my life? No. Now as an adult, my heart wells up in love that my God is not a taskmaster who wants me to feel as though life is a drudgerous duty. He delights in giving me the joy to serve Him. If I miss the joy, I have come to realize, the problem lies in my perspective of the situation, not because the joy is not there. He promises that in His presence there is fullness of joy. I must give thanks to my Savior who allowed me to grow up in an adopted country, which allowed me to be the beneficiary of blessing after blessing as the result of His amazing grace in my life.

Chapter Sixteen

Through It All

Mu Yonso

The Italian jumbo jet airplane pulled onto the tarmac at Njili Airport in Kinshasa, the capital city of the Democratic Republic of Congo, on December 8, 1978. It had been an exhausting trip for our family of five. We children were anxiously waiting to see what was on the other side of the bolted jet door. We had left behind snow in Detroit and were all carrying our heavy winter coats. Our dad had told us it never snowed in

The point of no return—boarding our first flight to Congo, 1978. Left to right: Nicol, Nancy, Shawn.

Congo. We could hardly imagine this, especially with the arrival of Christmas being just two weeks away. We knew this Christmas would be different, but we reassured ourselves that the presents would still find their way under whatever tree would be there on Christmas Day.

The flight attendants were told to make final preparations to open the door, which would end our journey from America to this new country we were to come to know as our home. In contrast to our anticipating this new life as an adventure, our mother's adrenaline was coursing through her veins at the thought of where our journey was ending. She knew that on the other side of that door was a foreign country very unlike the one she had just left. Our excitement as children was borne out of youthful ignorance and naïveté to the difficult adjustments to this new culture that lay ahead for our family. My mother was afforded no such luxury. She had spent many hours during the last two days of our trip thinking of all she had given up to be on that airplane.

The doors to the Boeing 747 were opened and the temperature in the airplane immediately swelled to an uncomfortable level as the blistering heat of the rainy season rushed in to extinguish the comfort of the air-conditioned cabin. As my mother emerged from the jet, the only thing more staggering than the heat was the unpleasant smell that found its way into her nostrils. Three months pregnant with her fourth child, the smells made her nauseous. Already frightened about the fact that no one in the country knew we had arrived, her apprehension rose dramatically within seconds of leaving the airplane.

What am I doing here? God, You know that I am here only out of sheer obedience. Where are my children going to sleep tonight? How are we going to even get there, because no one even knows we have arrived? I must be dreaming. Lord, You know I never wanted to be a missionary! Is Your choice for me to be here some cruel joke? I don't know the language, but most of all, I just want to get out of here! These thoughts came through my mother's mind one after another as we walked toward the chaos of the airport terminal. They made every step toward her new life more difficult than the one she

The last family picture before we went to Congo in 1978. Left to right (standing): *Jim, Shawn.* Left to right (sitting): *Todd, Nancy, Nicol.*

had just taken. She wished she could change her one-way ticket to a round-trip and get out of the nightmare she felt she was living.

My mother had no lofty ideas of a rosy path following the Lord's calling on her life. She had faithfully served alongside my father in a church in Detroit for thirteen and a half years before they had stepped out in faith when my father began a ministry in music evangelism. The move from Detroit to Hesperia, Michigan, had been challenging, but she had been able to trust that the Lord had led them every step of the way. Just a year earlier, we had lost all of our earthly possessions in a fire. Still, when my father's remark after their initial phone conversation was "Babes, the Lord gives and the Lord takes away," she had said, "Blessed be the name of the Lord." In the trauma of the fire, she had been confident of the Lord's guidance and presence.

Although my father had immediately felt the Lord's call to return to the country of his birth after the fire, my mother had felt no such call. She reminded both him and the Lord that she was the only one in the chapel at Detroit Bible College who had deliberately walked out of the room at the invitation by the speaker to commit to foreign missions. Her mind was filled with despair that the Lord had seemed to forget her adamant refusal to become a missionary during that chapel service. And on top of all of this, she found herself on the continent she had most feared going to as a missionary—Africa.

Her fear almost choked her when she contemplated all the unknowns. She was confident that to be a real missionary, one of us children would have to die a horrible death— perhaps of malaria or a poisonous snakebite—and be buried in African soil. My mother loved pretty clothes and wearing make-up. Her image of a true woman missionary did not match with her desire to keep up with fashion. She and my father had visited Congo, then the Belgian Congo, in 1969, and knew how remote our final destination on the mission station of Nkara-Ewa would be. Going through customs at Njili Airport was even more unnerving than she had feared it would be. People's stares and constant incomprehensible chatter cast a shadow of despair and isolation over my mom.

The mission station of Nkara-Ewa was our final destination three months after our arrival in Congo. Loneliness settled in as my mother's constant companion, especially when we arrived and saw evidence that our new home had been inhabited by seven families along with their livestock. My mother made a calendar of 1200-plus days until furlough. Her favorite time of the day was crossing each day off the calendar. We children would find her in her bedroom crying nearly every day from the loneliness of her situation. I remember many times when she would sob and say, "I hope you children don't remember me crying all the time in my room." The new language of Kituba, which had come easily to us children, was almost impossible for her to learn, especially when the Congolese would laugh at her American accent. Without being able to speak the language, the isolation she had continued to feel since our first day in Congo on the tarmac of the airport threatened to overwhelm her. She could only communicate with her husband and her children. Her days were spent weeping and looking after our baby brother, Jack, who had arrived safely six months into our first year in Congo.

Many might see my mother's first four years as a missionary as a waste of productivity. Many of us want to live vicariously through brave men and women who have lived overseas and have glorious stories to tell of how God brought thousands of men and women to Himself through their ministry. Very few churches would want a woman missionary to admit her constant loneliness and the fact

My favorite picture of two-year-old Jack, 1981.

she had not brought one person to Christ because she could not even communicate the gospel of Jesus Christ with the people she had been sent to.

Psalm 126:5–6 gives God's evaluation on my mother's first four years, which is vastly different from human judgment:

> *Those who sow in tears will reap with songs of joy. He who goes out weeping, carrying seed to sow, will return with songs of joy, carrying sheaves with him.*

My mother had voiced her concern about her grief, which was visible in her tears, and the effect it could have on her children. Her tears did affect her children, but not in the negative way she had feared. I have seen the harvest her tears of those early days have produced in countless lives, including mine. She knew the Lord had led our family to a strange, new country, even though she had not had the moment many would describe as God's calling on her own life to go. It was out of obedience she went. In those precious lonely hours, Jesus let her know she was His own.

Now Mom and Dad share the vision for Laban Ministries International. Somewhere along the pathway of obedience, the Lord gave my mother the passion and love she has today for the people of Congo. The joy has come also. Her calling to serve there is as much her own as it is our father's.

The amazing wonder of God is that He never looks at us as who we presently are, with our human fears and shortcomings, but what we can be through the power of the Holy Spirit. His ways are not our ways. We do not have to always like what He has called us to do; we just need to be obedient. Christ's transforming power allows us to accomplish things we once said we never could or never would. He has the ability to give us a love so deep for others that its depth can only be explained as supernatural. What causes fear in our human weakness is overcome through Him being our strength. The pathway of obedience often looks unappealing because we feel we do not have the ability to walk it. The joy comes in realizing He never asks us to walk where He has not gone before. It is through it all that we learn to trust in Jesus.

Chapter Seventeen

Hold On

Shimbana

". . . Weeping may endure for a night, but joy comes in the morning." —PSALM 30:5 (AMP)

We always had music in our home, whether we were singing or listening to it. Our dad had been in music evangelism for four years preceding our family's arrival as missionaries in the Congo. Each of us children had made an individual musical debut at the age of two on the platform of the church where our parents had served for thirteen years. We all learned early in life the power of music to inspire, encourage, or empathize with the listener.

We listened to many different styles of music, but some performers stood out as favorites. One album we listened to over and over again was Andrae Crouch's *Live at Carnegie Hall*. We sang our hearts out to "Through It All," "Till It Happened to Me," "I Don't Know Why Jesus Loved Me," "My Tribute," and of course, "The Blood Will Never Lose Its Power." The late 1970s praise music scene was dominated by the soulful, clear voice of Miss Evie Tornquist. We listened to her albums and cassettes until we wore them out. One of my sister's favorites was Evie's rendition of Jesse Dixon's song "Hold On," which she would rewind and sing to over and over again on the little portable cassette

Nicol in Congolese dress, 1980.

player we had. Nicol did not know then how powerfully God would use that song in her own life.

Our mother home-schooled Nicol, Todd, and me for

the first two years after our arrival in the Congo. As my sixth-grade year drew to a close, I started feeling an intense need to be with other English-speaking children. Knowing that addressing this need in my life would require me to board away from home, my parents reluctantly inquired about the possibility of my attending a small school for missionary children in the northwestern part of Congo. After much prayerful deliberation, my parents and I decided I would spend my seventh-grade year at Ubangi Academy. The school was located on the other side of a massive jungle of dense forest that spanned almost the entire six hundred miles between the school campus and our mission station. Because there were no roads between the two points, the school could only be accessed by airplane. This meant I would be coming home only every eight to ten weeks. Although I had more than a little trepidation as I left that August, great excitement surged through me over the adventure that lay ahead.

Because Nicol was in fifth grade at the time, and Todd was only in second grade, they stayed behind to continue their school lessons at home with our mother. The fact that we were the only English-speaking American family on our mission station had forced us, as siblings, to play together constantly. Nicol and I, being sisters only two years apart, were each other's closest friends. We only had each other in whom to confide our girlish secrets. The separation caused by my leaving for boarding school was wrenching and heartbreaking for both of us, but especially for Nicol, who was being left behind.

Soon after I left, Nicol came down with the first of many successive bouts of malaria. Carried in the bite of the female mosquito, malaria can sometimes affect one's vision, and Nicol was soon convinced she was going blind. Her greatest passion and hope at ten years old had been to excel as a figure skater. She realized she would never be able to see that dream fulfilled, as she now lived in a country that had temperatures so hot and humid that our kerosene

Nicol and her devoted pet monkey, T.D., 1981.

refrigerator's freezer could not produce a single cube of solidly frozen ice. Nicol soon sank into a very real and deep depression.

More than any other song she listened to that dark year, "Hold On" brought her the greatest comfort and hope. All my parents could do that year for Nicol was pray for her and reassure her that she was in God's hands even if she didn't feel Him holding her there. More than once we all questioned why God had brought us to the isolation and starkness of bush living. God confirmed many times that He had brought us to Congo and that this was the center of His will for our family. Instead of His will being a place of happiness and comfort, we were experiencing profound homesickness, separation from one another, and many tears. Through all of those disturbing emotions was the irony of the assurance that He had deemed those experiences for us for a purpose we could not see at the time.

The patriarch Jacob of the book of Genesis wrestled with a man on the eve of a terrifying event when his world was on the verge of collapse. Jacob knew this was no ordinary man and held on to him tenaciously during the time they were together. In the process of wrestling with this being, Jacob was, undoubtedly, knocked to the ground and did not leave the encounter without a limp that he would have for the rest of his earthly life. Although the wrestling took all night, something in Jacob made him know he had to hold on to the man until the one with whom he wrestled blessed him. Jacob was called an overcomer by God Himself because of his tenacity and was given a new name. He was profoundly changed for his perseverance.

Nicol also came out of that year when she was ten years old profoundly changed. Only God knew then how He would use that troubling year to develop empathy in Nicol for other people's pain. I believe Nicol's ability to communicate hope to the listener of her own music came out of the year she struggled to cope with fear and heartache as a young girl. The crucible of suffering purifies. The Lord completely healed her body and vision. Perseverance always brings reward. Nicol could not sing today with the depth of empathetic emotion contained in her vocal interpretation of the music without believing in the goodness of the One with whom she wrestled that year in Congo. God knew she had to live at the tender age of ten what she now sings in order to minister to others. Her music would be one-dimensional otherwise, lacking the God-given power He has anointed the music with to bring comfort to those who listened to it.

Newlyweds Greg and Nicol Sponberg in Ireland, 2003.

Only Jesus Christ can redeem that which has the power to devastate us and make us bitter. Perhaps even more amazing is that He chooses to bless us by using our own pain to bring comfort to another's broken heart. In our greatest weakness, He shows His mighty strength. Some-times life feels like a wrestling match, with one blow coming right after another. Nothing is more discouraging than when we have been obedient to the will of God and life feels as though we are getting mud on our face from being knocked to the ground. It is easy to start wondering if the fight is worth the effort it sometimes demands. In those times we must cling to and believe the words of the apos-tle Paul:

> *Therefore we do not lose heart. Though outwardly we are wasting away, yet inwardly we are being renewed day by day. For our light and momentary troubles are achieving for us an eternal glory that far outweighs them all. So we fix our eyes not on what is seen, but on what is unseen. For what is seen is temporary, but what is unseen is eternal.* —2 CORINTHIANS 4:16–18

Chapter Eighteen

You Raise Me Up

Nge Telemisa Mono

I n January 1979, our parents started a small Bible institute in the heart of the province of Bandundu. Congo, or Zaire, as the country was called at that time, is made up of nine provinces. Convinced that the way to make lasting change in the lives of Congo's poor was to train men and women in the Word of God so that they could take the gospel back to their own villages, they started the training with seven men in a small, one-room building. Three years later, after completing courses in such subjects as hermeneutics, systematic theology, and Old and New Testament survey, the first class of Laban Bible Institute was graduated and started seven new churches in their home villages. From those humble beginnings over twenty-five years ago, Laban Bible Institute has graduated more than five hundred men and women. Most have gone back to their villages to bring the gospel to their own people.

Because the country has such poor roads, these pastors and evangelists faced the daunting reality that only those villages they could personally travel to on foot would be able to hear the life-changing message of Jesus Christ. In 1997, friends from the United States promised money for a radio station that would allow those villages that had never been reached to hear the gospel. In 2004, the Lord allowed a three-hundred-foot radio tower to be erected on the mission station of Nkara-Ewa on East Hill.

Radio Nkembo (Radio Glory) on East Hill at Nkara-Ewa.

There were no cranes for use by those constructing the tower, so the tower had to be erected by hand, piece-by-piece, three hundred feet in the air. The fact that all the radio equipment arrived on the mission station intact and no one was injured during the tower's erection was nothing short of a miracle. As the last piece of the tower was placed on the top of the three-hundred-foot structure, the eyes of one of the radio construction team members fell on the small, twisted body of a Congolese woman named Afi.

Afi's legs were so deformed that she had to drag them behind her body as she used the backs of her wrists to slowly propel herself forward along the ground. She had no wheelchair to allow her the luxury of even seeing the world from a sitting position. The Congolese do not pen up their animals, but let them roam freely around their living quarters and deposit their filth indiscriminately. This was what Afi's view of the world had been all of her life, as she had to drag herself through whatever was in her path.

The man on the radio tower construction team decided that day that Afi should have a different view of the world. Using a harness as a seat, Afi was strapped securely and lifted up high above everyone on the ground. I cannot imagine her exhilaration at what this height allowed her to view. All she had known was the filth and muck that she had been forced to drag herself through all of her life. Afi was now raised above her surroundings, which must have looked very different from that vantage point.

Jesus said in John 12:32, "But I, when I am lifted up from the earth, will draw all men to myself." The Son of God became a human being so that He would be able to identify with our sorrow. Christ was lifted up from the earth on a cross, taking on Himself the penalty of our sin, so that He could then draw us to Himself.

Afi, experiencing the exhilaration of her new view.

Without Christ's power and presence in our lives, we are all as crippled as Afi. How small has our vision of God's power in our lives become because we have felt little hope that the muck of our lives will ever change? We can easily forget He is the same God who delights in showing His glory to those who will believe Him. The God we serve today is the One who made a way for His people to cross the Red Sea on dry land, let a shepherd boy kill a giant, and conquered death itself by raising His Son, Jesus Christ, to life.

> *You give me your shield of victory; you stoop down to make me great.* —2 SAMUEL 22:36

Have we lived in the muck and mire so long that we no longer believe there is a way out of the mess that our lives may have become? Jesus, the King of angels and the beloved One of His Father, stoops down to make us poor sinners great. Christ condescends to mere human beings. He invites us to trade our sorrow for joy and our mourning for His gladness. Afi was able to be lifted above the filth of her surroundings and was given a new view of her world. Christ longs to do the same for us as He stoops down to raise us up.

The Story Goes On...

Afterword

Do you see what this means—all these pioneers who blazed the way, all these veterans cheering us on? It means we'd better get on with it. Strip down, start running—and never quit! No extra spiritual fat, no parasitic sins. Keep your eyes on Jesus, who both began and finished this race we're in. Study how he did it. Because he never lost sight of where he was headed— that exhilarating finish in and with God—he could put up with anything along the way: Cross, shame, whatever. And now he's

Laban and Marcella Smith's descendants, 2007. Left to right (starting in front row): First row: *Jordyn Lantz, Jenna Lantz.* Second row: *Chase Lantz, Shawn Lantz, Jim Smith, Nancy Smith, Nicol Sponberg* (holding Summer Sponberg). Third row: *Rob Lantz, Greg Sponberg.* Fourth row: *Todd Smith* (holding daughter Sarah Kate Smith), *Jack Smith* (holding daughter Bella Smith). Fifth row: *Abby Smith, Angie Smith, Ellie Smith, Molly Smith.*

there, in the place of honor, right alongside God. When you find yourselves flagging in your faith, go over that story again, item by item, that long litany of hostility he plowed through. That will shoot adrenaline into your souls!

HEBREWS 12:1–3 (*THE MESSAGE*)

About Laban Ministries International

Rooted in seventy years of missionary experience, **Laban Ministries International** finds its home in the heart of the African continent in the Democratic Republic of Congo (D.R.C.). What began in 1979 with seven Congolese students in a one-room Bible school, has grown into a thriving, vibrant ministry with over five hundred graduates from the school's three-year, two-level program. The heartbeat of Laban Bible Institute is evangelism. Located in Congo's heaviest populated Bandundu Province, an area the size of the state of Texas, the students see the Scriptures come alive in theory and practice as they reach out to multiple thousands of fellow nationals weekend after weekend. Mass evangelism is accomplished through the showing of *The Jesus Film,* as well as through the more than two hundred fifty new churches started by Laban graduate pastors. The students are trained in a one-on-one approach in evangelism as well.

The newest, most cost-effective evangelistic arm of Laban Ministries was inaugurated in 2004. Radio Nkembo (Radio Glory), comprised of a three-hundred-foot tower along with a modest studio, broadcasts the gospel of Jesus Christ daily. Professors, pastors, and staff of Laban Ministries

International enthusiastically preach the Gospel of Jesus Christ. The broadcasts also include playing Christian music, the teaching of the Scriptures, along with health programs and the sharing of personal testimonies. Radio Nkembo broadcasts are heard ten hours a day, seven days a week, to a potential audience of five million people. The Women's Literacy Center began in 2004 with thirteen students. The program grew to thirty-two students in 2005. The center anticipates over fifty women in the program as of the 2008 academic year. Many are now reading for the very first time, exchanging ignorance caused by illiteracy for dignity and self-respect.

The next three projects on the horizon are water wells for Congo, a hospital for over two hundred thousand people with no health-care facility, and a Bible for every home in the Bandundu Province. For more information about Laban Ministries International or to become a ministry partner, please visit the ministry's Web site at www.labanministries.org. All monetary gifts to the ministry are tax-deductible.